CELEBRATING MARRIAGE

II

Encouragement for the Journey

Twenty-Three Couples Tell Their Marriage Stories

Compiled by Rebecca F. Duke

I would like to thank all the contributors. Except for light editing, the stories are presented as submitted.

Published by

Encouraging Word Press, Inc.

Amelia Island, Florida

www.encouragingwordpress.com

Table of Contentment

DEDICATION

I know no couple who married at ages 15 and 16; had a solid marriage for over fifty-six years, weathered many challenging times; had eleven children and around 50 grandchildren/ great-grandchildren; and enjoyed life to the fullest. That special couple is my sister, Florinette, and her husband, Jimmy Renfrow, whose story is a blessing to share. Florinette was South Carolina's Mother of the Year in 2002. As my older sister, she was like another mother to me and the model of love, determination, encouragement, and deep faith. I dedicate this book to you, Jimmy and Florinette, with the hope that young couples will read your story and receive the blessings of your commitment and dedication.

SPECIAL THANKS

Thank you, writers, for sharing your memories via your inspiring stories. I hope that you enjoyed the adventure as much as I enjoyed reading your treasures. Your gifts will be passed down and enjoyed for generations.

Thank you, my dear husband and daughter, for giving me the chance to chase my dreams again.

INTRODUCTION

If marriage took only love, my first marriage would not have ended in divorce. I am blessed with a second marriage of twenty-five years, having met a committed man, and having learned that success takes two people's full effort. The good news is that there are guides in this effort.

I am not an expert. Having now been in a supportive marriage, I know that each commitment has its own mapping. However, I have learned there are commonalities among couples. I want to share these commonalities which have helped many marriages last. Using personal stories, taking tips from young and older couples (marriage tips follow each story), you can use their helpfulness to begin, confirm, renew, or solidify your marriage commitment.

I started this collection of stories for my daughter, nieces, and nephews. I wanted to give them a legacy of our family marriages. As this dream unfolded, I included friends' marriages. I asked couples to write about how they met, the proposal, and the wedding. To cover the highlights of the rest of their marriage, I asked them for five to ten helpful marriage tips.

My first book, entitled *Celebrating Marriage*, unfolded after reading the uplifting, funny, and amazing coincidences in my family's and friends' marriage stories. I became more intrigued as I saw the commonalities of the marriage tips.

To date, I have collected over sixty-five marriage stories with over

1,500 years of married life, over two hundred marriage tips and over sixty marriage quotes. Putting forty-two stories in my first book and twenty-three in this second book, I have begun unfolding a new dream—spreading the marriage messages nationwide.

I believe that celebrating marriage is more than celebrating divine togetherness. It is embracing the process of mutual forgiveness, understanding, and patience with each other as human beings. It is honestly expressing feelings without fear of rejection, agreeing to disagree, and readily admitting mistakes and poor choices of words. It is letting each other retreat to cave or castle without feeling abandoned. And when children come along, it is doubling all that. No— quadrupling it.

Marriage is celebrating a partnered comfort-zone, memorable moments, unforgettable joys, family/friend blending, prayer time, and healing humor. Sprinkling marriage with love, respect, commitment, honor, humor, wisely chosen words, courage, commitment and prayer, eases the challenge of daily commitment and years of togetherness.

Many of us have been hungry to find a person who will share our life celebrations and struggles; one who will stay the course. From where does this hunger come? When I was young, I read in the Bible about being "equally yoked with a partner." I did not understand it fully. Now I know that being equally yoked (2 Corinthians 6:14), feeding the "hunger," takes more than belief in a philosophy or a religion. It takes studying relationships that have worked.

I decided to study the life of Jesus, from whose life I extracted many lessons for my marriage. Jesus stayed in constant contact with His heavenly Father. He drew people's attention because He was a communicator. He was self-sacrificing but held to His beliefs. He withstood hatred as He expressed love. He was at times physically uncomfortable as He spread His comfort. He took time to pray, meditate, and reflect during His busy schedule.

Jesus' verbal reaction to anger was to stay calm and use wise words as often as possible. He emphasized family/friendship and personal connectedness as He traveled with His disciples and embraced crowds. Jesus taught healing instead of dissension and divisiveness. He supported goodness and fought evil. He was a couple's best example of commitment to God, then to each other, and finally, to others.

Equally yoked? Does that not sound somewhat tedious, young readers? Going through life making the same decisions? Yuck! Going through life feeling the same way about situations? Humph! Going through life uttering similar words? Dull! Wouldn't life be boring if we were like twins in every way: spiritually, emotionally, intellectually, physically, socially, and soulfully? We are made differently for a reason and that reason is to learn and grow through the differences. Our likenesses are the glue that makes this effort possible. A couple's growth is amplified and expedited when God's guidance is invited.

Jesse and I invite God into our relationship daily because we believe that commitment to each other is a path that God, Jesse, and I must travel together. Believing God wants to grow us gives us comfort in difficult discussions. Jesse says that I am forthright. I say I must be as honest as possible, though sometimes I show weakness in my wording and timing. However, I know we are learning and growing as a couple. I forgive my missteps, move positively forward, knowing it takes persistence.

Take your time in reading these stories, digest the tips that are meaningful, enjoy the quotes, and grow closer in an unexpected way with your partner. Spread the word that there are many healthy relationships out there. Share this book with young friends considering marriage and married couples considering divorce.

SHARE YOUR STORY

I celebrate these stories and lives. True stories are what people want. So, more stories are forthcoming. Imagine! A tidal wave of marriage success stories for you and thousands of others who are single, married, or divorced. Catch the wave.

Send me your story and those of your friends and family. Email me at jessebecky@comcast.net to get simple, writing instructions that make the effort, effortless. I will personally help you collect stories and encourage the writers. You will help bind legacies now and for generations to come. You will be blessed. The world will be blessed.

A good marriage is the union of two good forgivers.

-Ruth Graham Bell

Falling for Her Fast

Michael and Annie Ackerman
Married June 22, 1998
Santa Fe, New Mexico

Annie and I both had marriages earlier in our lives. She had been single for over twenty years and I, for over ten years. Neither of us was really looking for another mate. I think that "running the show the way we liked it" had become just the way for both of us.

Along came Bob and Nancy Sibley, mutual friends of ours, who thought that we would be great for each other. I have to give them an "A" for persistence, because it literally took months of Nancy prodding Ann and of Bob prodding me before our fateful first date actually took place. I was immediately taken with her. Unfortunately, she did not see it the same way. She actually left me that first evening with the "I don't feel well" line, and she went home. Guess I really know how to impress a woman, right? I was crushed!!

But I was not deterred. I waited the appropriate two or three days (did not want to seem too eager) and called her again. The second attempt went much better. Now, I was on a roll and falling for her fast. Unfortunately, I soon found out that she and Nancy had been planning a trip together to, of all places, New Zealand! Within two weeks of meeting the love of my life, she disappears to the other side of the earth.

No phone number and no email address (this was fifteen years ago as of 2009). I was crushed again.

After several weeks, the ladies did return to our side of the planet. We dated for about a year and a half and were engaged for a year. In May of 1998 we were making plans to attend the wedding of a daughter of some good friends in Santa Fe, New Mexico. Since we were going to be in the company of friends, I asked Annie if she would like to get married in Santa Fe. Without telling any of our home-town friends in Fernandina Beach, Florida, what we were up to, we traveled to Santa Fe.

We waited several days after attending our good friend's daughter's wedding. We were married on June 22, 1998, in the state capital court-house by one of the Supreme Court justices of New Mexico.

After all these years, hardly a day passes that we do not both say "I love you" to each other. We both chip in and do housework, yard work, cooking, caring for the pets, making sure that the other has taken their vitamins, and so on. In other words, we are still good friends who share not only good times, but also the day-to-day work duties that no one may want.

Marriage Tips:

1. Spend twenty to thirty minutes of quiet time together each day (not at dinner with the children nor watching TV). Just call it "private time" to talk with each other.

2. Talk with your spouse about things that the individual does not really want to talk about. For example, many couples may have different opinions on such matters as cooking, dressing properly (I'm so bad about this one), money management, housecleaning, exercise, eating, drinking habits, picking up after oneself (oops, that's me again), turning off the lights and TV, and the list goes on and on.

3. Even the slightest hint of criticism (although it is meant to be constructive criticism) will sometimes create a negative and defensive attitude from the other. (If you have been married longer than a week, you know what I'm talking about.) My tip on this touchy time would be that, in most cases, you should just let it go. None of us are perfect. (However, I got an email from a friend recently saying that her marriage had ended because of religious differences. He thought he was God, she didn't.) Notice that I said "in most cases," let it go. There are some instances where it's worth the effort to make a stand. These would be involving the health, welfare, and safety of your mate. Examples: smoking, obesity, driving too fast, etc. It would be foolish to just sit by and watch your loved one destroy his or her life, and not make any attempt to help. It may be wise to get professional advice before stepping into this briar patch all by yourself. The word "tact" comes to my mind in these cases. Tact is defined as "skill in situations in which other people's feelings have to be carefully considered." Obviously, the last thing you want to do is be inconsiderate toward someone you love.

4. Here are a few more mine fields where one needs to step carefully. *Never* yell or even raise your voice at your spouse. *Never* use four-letter words (unless it's LOVE) during difficult discussions. *Always* sit close or even hold your spouse while you talk. *Be sincere.* (If this advice is helpful, there will be less scarring… AND there will be no need for a hospital visit. ☺)

There is a proverb, "As you have made your bed, so you must lie in it," which is simply a lie. If I have made my bed uncomfortable, please God, I will make it again.

-- G.K. Chesterton

Buried Car Keys

Lyn and Adrienne (Holman) Anderson
Married August 8, 1959
Timmonsville, South Carolina

I'll never forget my first date with him. He arrived at 6:30, came in, spoke to my parents, and then we left for dinner at McCain's Restaurant in Florence, South Carolina. We talked incessantly all the way there, but nothing was mentioned about what we would order. I assumed that he would have a steak with all the trimmings, so my taste buds were already thinking "steak." I nearly fainted when the waiter came to take our order and without changing his expression Lyn said, "I'll have tomato soup and water." From that moment on I knew that my life would always be filled with unexpected surprises! Needless to say,we did end up with steak!

The next day when Ella (my parents' cook, maid, baby-sitter, and a person who always had time to listen to me when I wanted to "talk") came to work, the very first thing I said to her was, "Ella, I'm going to marry Lyn Anderson, but he doesn't know it yet!"

For a year we dated nearly every night. Sometimes we would just sit and talk in my den. But whatever we did it was always fun and I can still remember how I looked forward to seeing him each time.

Lyn and I both finished two years of college. He had gone to Clemson College in Clemson, South Carolina, and I had gone to Converse College in Spartanburg, South Carolina.

We got married August 8, 1959, in the Timmonsville United Methodist Church. If you remember, I said my life would always be filled with unexpected surprises. Our wedding day was no exception to this. It was fifteen minutes before the wedding was to begin and Lyn was nowhere to be found. I was beginning to feel like the bride with no groom. Three minutes before the processional was to begin, Lyn came flying through the door, all out of breath, as he explained that his baby sister, Abigale, had buried his car keys in the yard while he was dressing. Once the processional started, everything moved along as planned.

After our honeymoon we returned to the Peniel community in Timmonsville to live. Lyn farmed and had a dairy. Our two boys were born while we were living on the farm. (Speaking of boys being born, my dad, Dr. D.O. Holman, had delivered my husband when he was born!) Many days Dad would stop by the dairy barn and "visit" while Lyn milked the cows.

We eventually had the opportunity to move to Orangeburg, South Carolina, to run a cotton gin and farm supply operation. While we were living there we were introduced to the Tennessee walking horse. Both of us had always loved horses and dogs, but now we developed a love for showing horses. The horse shows we visited were family oriented. Lyn, both of our boys, and I would all show our horses and then we would "tailgate" with our friends each Saturday during the show season.

The Lord can speak to us in so many ways. Lyn and I and our two boys moved back to Peniel, where we were active in the Peniel Baptist Church. I played the organ and he sang in the choir. During the invitation hymn on June 13, 1971, Lyn came out of the choir, told the minister something, and left the sanctuary. It was after the end of the hymn that the minister announced that Lyn had shared with him that he felt the Lord was calling him to be a minister. When I finished playing, I went to the pastor's study to find Lyn. He looked at me and said, "What do you think about that?" I told him I had been expecting it for over a year. From that moment on there was never a dull moment in our home. Attending night schools and seminaries, we both became ordained ministers.

The Lord has blessed me in so many ways. He has given me a husband who helps me and supports me in everything I do. He is a loving father, still my sweetheart, my lover, my mentor in the ministry, and my very best friend. The Lord has truly blessed us in a mighty way. I'm thankful that Lyn and I have each other. The Lord made him so special.

None of us knows how long we will be on the earth, so I am thankful for each day and for the joy I get from being with Lyn. We have had the pleasure of raising four children: Linwood, Neal, Adrienne E., and Summerlyn.

Marriage Tips:

1. Keep a prayer and praise journal each day to help you remember how many blessings you have each day.

2. Let the Prayer of Jabez be a part of your daily prayers:

   - Thank the Lord for all His blessings.

   - Ask for new territory.

   - Ask for God's strength.

   - Ask for God to keep you away from evil.

3. Always be supportive of each other.

4. Never lose your sense of humor.

5. Give your spouse a surprise present even if there is no specific reason. It does not have to be big or expensive.

6. Take the time to go out to eat—even if it is to Hardee's or Burger King. The break will be good for both of you.

7. You can never say "I love you" too much!

Real giving is when we give to our spouses what's important to them, whether we understand it, like it, agree with it, or not.

-- Michele Weiner-Davis, <u>Divorce Busting</u>

"Spacing"
During Space Odyssey, 2001

Frank and Joanne Boria
Married September 6, 1969
Newport, Rhode Island

The year was 1966. I had moved to the beautiful state of New Hampshire from my hometown, Newport, Rhode Island, to be with my sister. But after three months, I hadn't met anyone interesting, was bored, and was ready to move back home. My sister quickly had her boyfriend arrange a blind date to keep me there. Well, now we're cooking! I thought I needed a new look so I went back to Newport and cut my waist-length hair into a chic new short bob and was quite pleased with the results.

When my sister's doorbell rang I was ecstatic to see this handsome Italian guy named Frank. He said, "Hi, is Joanne home?" I said, "I *am* Joanne", and the next words out of his mouth were, "What happened to your hair?" (He had seen a picture of me with long hair.) Well, not surprisingly, it was not love at first sight! We went to the movie *Space Odyssey, 2001*, and came out raving to each other about how cool it was. Months later we would laugh as neither of us had the slightest clue as to what it was about!

Thinking we would never see each other after a somewhat rocky start, we both relaxed and truly enjoyed getting to know each other. Surprisingly, he called me the very next day and we began learning to down-hill ski. We became really good friends and gradually over three years of dating, fell in love. We were both from loving Italian families and shared a deep Catholic faith, which really laid the foundation for our future life together. We didn't move in together, and yes, there's something to be said about the old-fashioned concept of saving yourselves for marriage. We truly trusted each other.

But keep in mind, Frank was quiet, shy and a little on the nervous side. When he finally got up the nerve to propose to me, he came up to my apartment and asked me out to dinner. Now, also keep in mind that I was not quiet, not the least bit shy and had just accepted an invitation to my sister's house for my favorite meal, *liver and onions*! Well, Frank right then and there popped the question. On the night I found out that Frank hated liver and onions, I accepted his precious proposal of marriage! To this day, every time Frank sees an ingenious way of proposing he tells me he wishes he had been more original. Little does he know that I wouldn't have changed a thing!

We were married in Newport, Rhode Island, on September 6, 1969, in the church where I had been baptized. What a pretty wedding. My dad who was a proud Italian, wanted big weddings for all his seven daughters, but had recently broken his back at work. Frank, who admired my father immensely, made sure that he and I saved money for our own wedding. This told me something about the man I was about to marry. Dad beamed the whole day of the wedding.

Over the next forty years we have had four wonderful children, who have given us six precious grandchildren, and life has been good! Did we have any problems? You bet we did. There was glue that held us together. With God as our co-pilot and a sense of humor, we made it through rough times with flying colors.

Frank, who was a government inspector for the Department of Defense, turned out to be very handy with his hands and remodeled two homes for us in Maine, which enabled us finally to build our dream house on Amelia Island, Florida. I, who loved children and still do, opened a home day care and became "Miss JoJo." I helped raise over one hundred precious little angels here in Fernandina Beach. What a joy to see one of these angels—now towering over my head—come up to me in Publix and give me a big "huggy bear" as we used to call them. What a blessing.

This September we will celebrate our fortieth anniversary and we are planning a trip to Sicily. If we remember, we met on a blind date, and although we knew that we were both Italian, the surprising part was that both of our ancestors had come from little towns in Sicily only an hour away from each other! Amazing or what?

Marriage Tips:

1. Lighten up and enjoy each other.

2. Respect is so imperative in a relationship. We truly cherish each other.

3. We did not want to argue in front of our children, so at the beginning of our marriage we tried to discuss our problems in private, and we consciously tried to be cheerful and verbally supportive of each other.

4. This did not always work out, but we set the tone in our marriage by trying to think before we spoke, making sure those words were gracious and tender (for tomorrow you may have to eat them).

5. While raising our children, we were a team. We were tough but fair with our children and we did not try to be their buddies for we were The Parents.

6. We used to have a paddle on the wall with the children's names on it. If they misbehaved, we asked them to get the paddle. That is all they

needed to hear, AND we never used it.

7. As a couple, we expected a lot from our children and they aspired to give it to us. Our kids grew into responsible adults and now we truly enjoy their friendship.

8. "Life is a journey, not a destination!" These words written by Ralph Waldo Emerson are so true! So, enjoy the ride!!

For a marriage to have any chance, every day at least six things should go unsaid.

-- Author Unknown

I Know the Plans I Have For You (Jeremiah)

Keith and Claire (Renfrow) Darnell
Married May 21, 1988
Dillon, South Carolina

Many times in our lives, we make our own plans and ask God to join them, rather than cling to the Bible verses in Jeremiah that say, "I know the plans I have for you, says the Lord ..." What I have learned over the years is that God wants us to wait on Him, go where He is working, and then He will give us the desires of our hearts. I believe this with all my heart, because I have watched God change my heart into what He would have me desire. He knows what is best, if only we will listen. Experience has taught me this. I wish I could say I learned it straight from God's Word.

In 1986, I decided I was going to get married, begin my career as a teacher, start a family, and live happily ever after. The problem was that I decided all this on my own. I was sure God would be pleased, but I didn't really ask Him. I knew God's Word enough to know that when a person is to be married, the person leaves his or her father and mother and … you know the rest. When opposition came from my family to the plans I had made, I assumed this was part of the process. I determined in my heart that I knew what I was doing.

The young man who asked me to marry him was a Christian, so I knew I was on the right track. I didn't know then, but I know now that I was settling for what I thought was God's best for me. I knew there were things in our personalities that were not very compatible, but I had heard, "If two people are exactly the same, one of them is not necessary." So, I went ahead with my plans, despite the warning from the people God had placed in my life to guide me.

Five weeks before I was to walk down the aisle, God set in motion a series of events that would change my life forever. While camping on a Tuesday night with a group of girls at Camp Pinehill in South Carolina, I was approached by Keith Darnell, the assistant director I had been working with all summer. Keith and I were very good friends, but I had found it very hard to be around him because of the awkwardness I felt as we worked together. He was loved by everyone he came in contact with, but I felt for some reason that I needed to stay away from him. He always joked with me and seemed to enjoy my company, but I felt uneasy about spending too much time around him. It seemed unnatural to me that I would feel so free to talk with him and enjoy our interaction so much when I was about to be married in a few weeks. I was determined not to step over the boundaries I felt were necessary in relationships with the opposite sex. However, one night on the trail to the campsite, I was thrown for a loop.

Keith walked with me to get some medicine for one of my campers back at the campsite. When we returned, he stopped short of the campsite and began to ask me a series of questions. He wanted to know why a person who was about to be married would choose not to wear her engagement ring and why she never talked about her upcoming wedding. I was about to tell him jokingly it was none of his business, when he proceeded to tell me that he loved me, wanted to spend the rest of his life with me, and that he did not want me to get married. In the moonlight I could see his face and could tell he was serious. As I turned to face him, even though my pride made it hard to admit, I realized that I, too, felt the same way. Although the moment was perfect and seemed like a fairytale experience, the reality in my mind was that it could not matter.

With what had just been shared between us, I still felt I was too far into my own plans to change my situation. As I shared with Keith that I was not strong enough to change my plight, he proceeded to tell me that God had told him during his first weekend at the camp that I was the one he would marry. Speechless, I listened, began to cry discreetly, and tried to gather my words. I told him I was unsure that I was doing the right thing, but I would be getting married in a few weeks, because I'd said I would. I had to carry through with my plans because it was right thing to do. I was confused by Keith's words, but I assumed this just might be a test to see if I really was ready to be married. I knew I was failing the test but didn't know how to fix it.

I left Keith standing there that night with full confidence that I would be married in a few weeks and the whole conversation we had had would fade away and be forgotten. Besides, I knew that the Bible had taught me that if God had told someone something about me, if it was true, He would have told me, also. I hadn't heard anything from God about this because I hadn't asked him.

I left camp that weekend very troubled, but determined to get myself together and finish planning my wedding. My dad approached me when I returned home and asked me if I would be willing to postpone the wedding until Christmas. My mom had fallen earlier in the summer, had broken bones, and was not even able to wear a dress at that time. He said he would pay for everything again if I would give her more time to recover. I walked out of the room and began to weep. I knew God would never allow me to go astray without giving me a way of escape, but I felt helpless. My sister followed me out the room and asked what was wrong. I told her I must not be ready to get married, but I knew I had to carry through with my plans. She volunteered to step in and take care of everything for me if I wanted her to.

One of the hardest things I ever had to do up until that point in my life was to break my engagement on the following evening. I knew I had made a mess of this young man's life by pretending I knew what God had planned for me. I sat on my back steps and asked God to forgive me for the mess I had made and asked Him to bless the young man I had just watched leave my yard. My dad found me on the back steps and told me he had never been as proud of me as he was then. What a blessing I felt to know I had a dad who loved me and was proud of me despite the mess from which I had just walked away. As I went to bed that night, I promised God that I would no longer chart the course for my life, but that I would only go where He was leading me from that time forward.

I was very unsure of the plans God had for me, but I knew what He didn't want for me. During the next few months, Keith decided he was not going to give up on me. He wrote me letters from school and shared a lot of wisdom from God's word that helped me understand the man I eventually would want to marry one day. He sent me a poem that I still remember today. It read, *"Everyone longs to be loved by someone, to have a deep relationship with another. But God, to a Christian says "no"! Not until you fully understand the love I have for you, can you really love another ..."* From that time on I made a decision to learn to love God with all of my heart, soul, mind, and strength. Then I knew I would be ready to be loved and love someone else in a way that God would be honored.

After the campfire on the final Thursday evening of the 1987 summer season at Camp Pinehill, Keith asked me to walk with him to the prayer garden before returning to my cabin. He began to talk with me about the symbolism of the cross and its relationship to man. He said that the vertical part of the cross symbolized man's relationship to God and how that should be first in our lives. He then explained that the horizontal part of the cross represented man's relationship with man. If we wanted to have a good relationship with each other, he said, we must always keep a strong relationship with God. Sitting on the garden's cross that night, Keith asked me to be his wife and to spend the rest of my life with him. He said he believed that God had a plan for us that was far more wonderful than we could imagine. Keith had already asked my dad's permission to marry and had received my parents' blessings.

On May 21, 1988, Keith and I were married at First Baptist Church in Dillon, South Carolina. After returning from our honeymoon, we began our ministry together as husband and wife at the camp where we had met, been engaged, and would eventually have our first two children. Our plans from that day until now have been to learn to love God more, so we can know how to love each other better. In doing so, we continue to learn how to better share His love with others whom He puts in our path each day.

God has blessed Keith and me with five beautiful children over the past twenty-one years. We have had the honor of serving Him in wonderful places, with awesome people, and in a variety of unique ways. Our journey to love Him more has led us to make friends and share His plan of salvation from the plains of Africa to the shores of Myrtle Beach, South Carolina. Through the years we have learned, "In everything give thanks, for this is God's perfect will for you in Christ Jesus" (I Thessalonians 5:18). By His grace we have been given "a hope and a future" (Jeremiah 29:11).

Marriage Tips:

*M*emorize scripture that shows you how to love your husband.

*A*lways keep your marriage a priority.

*R*egularly pray together for each other. There is so much encouragement in hearing your husband pray for you.

*R*emember why you married him. Forget what makes you wish you had not. ☺

*I*magine how you want to be loved and love him that way.

*A*rrange for a time for you to be alone at least every twenty years. ☺

*G*uard what you say to your husband. Praise him in public. Fuss at him at home.

*E*njoy your time together. Do not take each other for granted. Life is too short.

Chains do not hold couples together. It is threads, hundreds of tiny threads, which sew people together through the years.

-- Simone Signoret

The Scavenger Hunt Surprise

Johnny and Helen Dowbak
Married December 1, 2007
Clemson, South Carolina

Johnny and Helen met during their freshman year at Wofford College in Spartanburg, South Carolina. Helen and her sorority sister had been advised by a friend to invite these two "great guys" to the end of the year sorority formal. However, much to Johnny's dismay, Helen went with "the other guy."

Johnny and Helen's friendship began to bloom the following summer as they spent the summer together in Myrtle Beach on a campus ministry project. It was towards the end of the summer that Johnny developed feelings for Helen in a way that was more than "just friends."

The next semester, Johnny's "crush" on Helen was in full swing. She, on the other hand, had no clue and believed that Johnny was just fun to hang out with. She decided to ask Johnny to the next sorority party. She thought she would play a little joke when asking him. She decorated his car with balloons and a card, inviting him to the party. Johnny saw the amount of work that she put into decorating his car and mistakenly interpreted everything as the "sign" he needed to move forward—that Helen obviously felt the same way as he, right?! Wrong!

After several weeks of deliberation, Johnny decided that he was going to ask Helen to go out with him. He sat down with her and began going over how he felt about her, that he was convinced they should start dating. Helen was completely caught off guard and had not even contemplated the idea. By the time he finished giving his pitch, she did not know what to think but decided she would at least give it some thought. Obviously, Johnny figured it did not go very well.

After thinking, praying, and discussing it with a lot of her friends, Helen decided that it would be a good idea to begin dating Johnny. She enjoyed spending time with him and could not think of a good reason why they should not at least see each other.

As time went on their relationship grew, but it was not until they spent some time apart that their relationship really took the crucial next step. Helen spent four months studying abroad in Madrid, Spain, during the spring of her junior year. During her time away from Johnny, her feelings for him were affirmed and she realized that she could see a long-term future with him.

After graduating from college they continued dating, although it looked much different because they were no longer a five-minute walk from one another as they had been during their time in college. Helen moved back home to Clemson, South Carolina, to pursue her master's degree in accounting, and Johnny started working in Spartanburg, South Carolina. After a year of making the long hour-

and-a-half drive to visit her, Johnny realized he was ready to ask the "big question."

On July 7, 2007, Helen woke up and went to class as if it was any other day. However, when she returned home she was greeted with a flower and a riddle sitting on her kitchen table. Her heart skipped a beat, and she had a suspicion of what the day might bring. Johnny had organized a scavenger hunt throughout upstate South Carolina, stopping at some of their favorite spots and places where they had spent time together. Johnny also involved all of Helen's best friends (in the secret, coming proposal) and had her call each of them as part of the scavenger hunt. She enjoyed every minute of it despite a short downpour of rain! At the last stop of the scavenger hunt, she found Johnny waiting with ring in hand! When the question came, of course she said "yes"!

After a wedding in Clemson, on December 1, 2007, they spent their honeymoon in St. Lucia in the Eastern Caribbean. They currently live in Greenville, South Carolina.

Marriage Tips:

1. Continue to pursue one another in marriage as when the relationship was just beginning.

2. Pray together and for one another.

3. Communication is essential—be transparent and open.

4. Live within your means.

5. Go on trips together.

6. Live out the words of Paul in Ephesians—"Husbands love your wives, and wives respect your husbands."

7. Learn how to serve one another—and do it daily.

The first duty of love is to listen.

-- Paul Tillich

The Rose Garden
at Furman University

Allen and Samantha (Renfrow) Evans
Married December 16, 1995
Dillon, South Carolina

In January 1995, Allen Evans showed up with a friend at Bruton's Fork Baptist Church in Bennettsville, South Carolina, on a cold, Wednesday winter night. At the time I was in the middle of my first year of teaching and was living with my sister, Claire, and her family in the parsonage of this church. Claire's husband, Keith Darnell, was the pastor of the church. I had only planned to stay with them temporarily until I could find a roommate and an apartment, but I had not found a roommate yet. I had no idea that Allen would eventually end up being that "roommate" (in our marriage) or that he already owned a house with plenty of room for me (in our future).

When Allen called to ask me out on our first date, I would have said "no" if I had actually realized the immensity of the situation. We were going all the way to Myrtle Beach, South Carolina, to have dinner and attend the Carolina Opry with his parents, his brother and girlfriend, and all the folks who worked in the office of Southern Packaging Corporation, the Evans' family business. If we had not gotten along well, we would have had an awkward hour-and-forty-five-minute drive home!

We did get along well, though, and we spent time together nearly every day over the next few months. Our dates usually consisted of many meals of Hamburger Helper and string beans with the Darnell family and then countless viewings of the movie *Free Willy* with their children. We were well-chaperoned and had plenty of quality time to get to know each other! I knew right away that Allen was a pretty special guy.

It wasn't until July 1995 that Allen got the *full* Renfrow family (there are eleven brothers and sisters in my family) introduction at the annual family beach trip in Ocean Isle Beach, North Carolina, with *only* about seventy family members present. Ocean Isle had always been a special place for our family, and, coincidentally, the Evans family had owned a place near Ocean Isle since Allen was a little boy. I was twenty-three years old and out of school, so naturally everyone in the family was curious about how serious we were. I told them we were "just friends," which was the truth.

Naturally, I was surprised when a week later Allen offered me a diamond ring in the Rose Garden at Furman University (my alma mater) in Greenville. After only three months of dating, I was a little shocked, but it only took me about an hour to get around to saying "yes" after Allen promised me that my daddy had already given his permission. I like to take my time about things, but Allen makes up his mind pretty quickly! He assured me that I could take as long as I needed to plan the wedding since our "dating phase" had been somewhat short.

Five months later on December 16, 1995, we walked down the aisle of First Baptist Church in Dillon, South Carolina and shared our wedding vows. The wedding party of approximately forty people included eighteen of our favorite children, our nieces and nephews!

After a honeymoon in Jamaica, we came back home to Bennettsville. We scurried around doing Christmas shopping in the two days we had left before our first Christmas together.

Time passed as we settled in as "roommates," and I was sure that life would slow down a little. Little did I know that we would be preparing our home for another little "roommate" in the months ahead! The special miracle of a baby was to be our blessing.

"Two are better than one, because they have a good reward for their labor; for if they fall, one will lift up his companion." Ecclesiastes 4:9

Marriage Tips:

1. The firm foundation for every home is Jesus Christ.

2. Love is not just an emotion; it is a deliberate choice.

3. Apologize, even if you do not think you are wrong and you think your spouse is …

4. Never criticize your spouse's family.

5. Do not go to bed angry with your spouse. You won't sleep well.

6. Encourage your spouse to have hobbies.

7. Always remember what made you fall in love with your spouse. Focus on the strengths of your spouse, not the weaknesses.

8. Giving in is sometimes a good idea.

9. Giving up is never an option.

The goal is to have a conversation so that you can have another conversation tomorrow.

-- Unknown

The New Girl
and the Country Boy

Russell and Lucy Ford
Married June 16, 1990
Lake View, South Carolina

Well, my social life had never been very colorful. I guess you could say I was *not* your typical teenage girl going to parties and having the millions of crushes like all of my friends. I never dated anyone in high school but always had a date when prom time came around. It seemed that boys would pop out of the woodwork to ask me out just for a special occasion. My senior year, I had to make a choice between three boys who had asked me to my final high school formal. I ended up going with Mike … about as exciting as a doorknob. It never panned out and we both went our separate ways in life.

The next time I even had interest in someone was in college studying in Scotland. I managed to "fancy" (as my Scottish friends called it) a quiet, textile chemist. He was so energetic, yet so introverted. I thought it was going to last because we were together for my last three years in college. I guess three was my magic number. But, alas, I found him very judgmental and almost embarrassed to "show me off." I was in Scotland and thought I had found the man of my dreams. I had visions of marrying in a foreign country and making Scotland my home. Not to be.

I traveled back to Connecticut and finally decided to continue my education at North Carolina State University in Raleigh. (Little did I know I was already in my home-state-to-be!) Graduating in 1988, I was on a job hunt. I finally picked a small, Southern town called Lake View, South Carolina. Funny how doors open and you just walk through on blind faith!

I went back North to Bridgeport, Connecticut, packed my worldly goods, and moved to Florence, South Carolina—all in about a week. My little red Toyota Tercel and I had ventured up and down I-95 one too many times. We knew it was time to take root somewhere, sometime soon. Indeed I did! Arriving at my new-found apartment, I wondered if it was *always* going to be this warm at ten p.m. in the South. The local bank thermometer read 101. I just knew I was going to melt in an instant!

My new position was as a woven textile designer at Carpostan Industries in Lake View. I figured folks commuted from Connecticut to New York every day. Surely I could do the same and learn to love Florence with all its surroundings. It was not to be. The drive was long, so I finally found a new abode in the "bustling metropolis" (ahem!) of Lake View, one mile from my work site. I had only commuted for three months—there is that magic number "three" again!

I had spent about ten years away from home just putting roots down wherever I ended up. I made friends all around the world and just longed for a constant companion. One day, I knew it would all come together. I just had to wait with "patience"—not exactly my style in this case. All of my friends were married and I was in this small, Southern town thinking my Prince Charming would find me....

Lo and behold, the tide turned. A courtship began! Little did I know my romance was right outside my work door. My phone rang one Friday and I was asked out on a *real* date! He said he would call me to firm plans that afternoon. I was so excited inside but stayed calm. I have always been the cautious type and surely didn't want to get my hopes up! You see, I have always been quite independent. Relationships seemed to crumble for so many of my friends and caused them many hours of pain. I really didn't wish that on myself. I had always been the shoulder others cried on and was comfortable in that role.

That Friday after work, I came home, waited for the phone to ring, and thought it never would. My "date" finally called again and asked if I could be ready in about one hour. I said, "Yes!" Funny, but one of my first thoughts was that I had no idea what to wear. Then ... I was going to "ride around" with some fella' from work ... just like that? I was anxious and excited but cautious just the same. I was like a teenager with butterflies taking residence in my stomach. It was like I had never been "out" before. Well, I hadn't in a while! I even forgot to ask him his name. Imagine!!

A brown Chevy S-10 pulled up at my humble abode. Out of the truck jumped a fella' whom I recognized from work but whose name I still did not know. He said, "Do you remember me? I work in the shop at Carpostan. My name is Russell Ford." I knew this was going to be an interesting evening. I was about to climb into this man's truck and had no idea where I was about to go. My mom always said to have a quarter for a phone call, just in case. Well, inflation had hit since my teenage years, so I had one dollar in change just for that purpose. ☺

So, the evening began. My first "real" date in several years and I was riding around the countryside in a *truck* with a man I hardly knew! We rode around for about three hours, stopping for a snack, talking, and comparing notes about our lives and what we had done in the past. Then, it occurred to me I had *no* idea where I was. I just had to trust that I would get home safely. And I did. Russell invited himself in, but I politely declined, thinking he could come back another time.

So, the courtship went. We dated for about a year, saving Friday nights for our night out "on the town." Fridays in Dillon, Lake View, Fair Bluff or Mullins were nothing but a quiet time just to relax and get to know each other better.

In December of 1989 there was a turnaround in our courtship. I had been pushed aside for another. I was stunned. Not understanding what had happened, I dove into my work and wondered how I could avoid him on the job and in this small town. As I reflect back, God knew best. He always does. I returned from a business trip in January and received the phone call that changed my life forever! "Lucy," he said. "Can you come over about 5 p.m.?" I told him, "No, but I will be there about 5:07." ☺ I left work at 5 p.m., needing time to cross the North Carolina/South Carolina state line, which was not too far away.

My little red Toyota traveled to Blackankle, North Carolina. I pulled up behind Russell Ford's singlewide mobile home. I just knew I never wanted to live in a mobile home but visiting was okay. I walked inside. Nothing special was said. I was escorted to the kitchen table. There on the placemat was a small box (the kind every girl dreams of receiving). Atop the box was a pretty red bow. I knew he had taken care to pick out whatever was inside. I wasn't going to get my hopes up but the thought of a "ring" did cross my mind. Lo and behold, in a floral setting of diamonds was an engagement ring, my engagement ring. I never thought this gift would *ever* come my way, especially from him, after our time apart.

Russell said, "How about Valentine's Day?" I immediately said,

"No, that's too soon. I need time to call my parents and plan the entire celebration." The plans were running through my head—a dress, the bridal party, the ceremony, the reception and more! Russell agreed to wait patiently and have a church wedding. I was ecstatic. I figured I would only be married once. I wanted to make it an occasion to remember.

I called my parents. They were ecstatic and started planning to come state-side from Saudi Arabia in the summer. Little did I know, my older brother was to be remarried. His fiancée and I had chosen the same date, June 16, 1990. Mom decided that I had first dibs on the date since this was my first marriage. I guess being the only daughter had its privileges!

I contacted my best friend of many years and asked her to be my matron of honor. She agreed and so the planning continued. I never really had help. My mom and dad were overseas and Russell's family had few opinions. I located a caterer in town and was so happy that she handled it all. I would call my mom occasionally for the next four to five months and update her. All was well.

My wedding dress fabric was Damascene silk brocade purchased in Syria on a family trip in 1979. My mom always knew I would marry. I asked her to send me the fabric. I picked three patterns, pieced them together and was elated when the dress was complete. I felt like a fairytale princess. I had longed for this day for years.

At the age of twenty-seven, older than my close, married friends, I was betrothed. Russell and I had the standard, big church wedding. Over four hundred invitations were sent out and out-of-town guests descended on this little Southern town. Everyone knew the *new girl* in town was getting married to the *country boy* from across the state line! The ceremony went off without a hitch and the reception was the highlight of the night. We had a never-ending buffet with dance music for five or so hours.

I was exhausted but ran on adrenaline for the next few days. We did not have honeymoon plans, but traveled to Massachusetts the next weekend for my brother's wedding. I guess that served as a honeymoon for us, only one week into our new life together.

After four years and one miscarriage, the Lord blessed us with our daughter, Hannah Sarah-Frances. She is an angel from above. God heard my prayers for a baby and fulfilled it in His time! Our marriage has been good. We have been blessed.

We had lived separate lives for so long. We came together. I accepted a whole new way of life when the city girl married the country boy. Now we live across the state line in North Carolina.

June 16, 2009, will mark our nineteenth anniversary. Russell is a mechanic with Pepsi-Cola and I am a night shift registered nurse. I think we manage well. Our schedules are opposite one another. We have our own time with Hannah as well as our family time. I always wanted to have six children and to marry a farmer. Fortunately, God has taken me down a different road. (Always, always turn to Him and He will direct your path.)

Marriage Tips:

1. Save yourself for the one you truly love. If you love your spouse, he or she will wait for marriage.

2. Marriage will not change either partner.

3. It is a major lesson in compromise and accepting differences.

4. Each partner has to give the other space and time to do his or her own thing.

5. Do not sweat the little things, for it is only wasted energy.

6. Have all your ways and means out in the open. Do not keep secrets from each other.

7. Trust your partner to the highest mountain. If there is no trust, to me there is no relationship.

8. Love your spouse for who he or she is, not what the person is. Russell never, ever judged me on the outside. I was always told my heart was

as big as Texas and that is why he married me.

9. Know you are beautiful in the eyes of your spouse.

10. Most of all, respect each other always. Respect will carry you far.

11. Communication is the cement of marriage.

It is not your love that sustains the marriage, but from now on, the marriage that sustains your love.

> *--Dietrich Bonhoeffer, writing to a   young bride and groom from his prison cell in Nazi Germany in 1943*

I'll Be Your Crying Shoulder

Robert and Rebecca (Powell) Hampshire
Married September 27, 2008
Bennettsville, South Carolina

While a senior in college three years ago (2006), I began to notice a pretty young lady from another school, who was the sister of one of my friends. I was friends with a lot of girls in my small Christian college and even went on dates with a few of them, but Rebecca was different. I began finding out as much as I could, and the more I found out, the more I wanted to know. After several emails to "test the waters," I got the nerve to call her.

Our conversations remained mostly casual until I found out that she was going to be in the area, so I invited her over to my house for a date. It was going to be the first time we met in person, so I did everything I could to make it special. I set out some new plates and fancy glasses, marinated some chicken, and even bought some sparkling grape juice for the occasion. When she arrived, I went out to meet her on the front porch; she was beautiful. Dinner went well, the chicken was her favorite dish, and the evening was filled with simple flirtation. She was casual and easy to get along with, which made her very easy to talk to. I was so excited about our new relationship, but after our first date, things did not really advance. Eventually, she found out that my roommate was her ex-boyfriend and we agreed that dating would be too difficult. Sadly, we quit talking.

For some reason, almost a year later, I randomly came across her picture. However, I had been quick to remove her number from my phone after we quit talking a year before. After ashamedly exchanging numbers, Rebecca and I began talking again. Our intentions were to let our relationship build slowly and naturally, but we began to get closer and closer; it was as if we were both different people after being separated for a year. We often found ourselves talking late into the night, and we met as much as we could. The time that we spent together was perfect, and I began to find ways to see her more and more.

That summer I drove to join her and her family at the beach for a few days. On one of the nights, we walked on the beach for a couple of hours. I wrapped my arms around her and we began to dance as I sang her a song, "I'll be your crying shoulder...." (Edwin McCain) It was a magical night.

After only seven or eight months of dating I started thinking that she was the one for me. During this time she was preparing to graduate college, and my job as an interim pastor was coming to an end. At probably the worst possible time financially and occupationally for both of us, I decided to propose! One May evening after a church basketball game, Rebecca and I drove back to my church in Simpsonville, South Carolina. As she stepped into the restroom, she thought that I was just grabbing a few things from my office; instead, I was getting a ring from my desk drawer. When she came out, I asked her to step into the darkened sanctuary with me for a second.

We walked down a candlelit aisle to the front of the room, where I directed her to sit on the front pew and I continued to the stage and picked up my guitar. As soon as I began to play, the lights were raised and several members of my church band, including a saxophonist, joined me. I sang, "I'll be your crying shoulder...." When I was finished, the band continued to play and I set my guitar down and motioned for Rebecca to come to the altar with me. I dropped to one knee, presented the ring to her, and asked her to marry me, to which she agreed. We bent down, prayed and asked God's blessing, and walked out of the sanctuary and into the gym where I had invited our friends to meet us for a party. It was a wonderful night.

The next months flew by while we tried to plan our wedding, which was difficult because neither Rebecca nor I could seem to find a job, and we had no place to live. In September 2008, I got a call from a pastor in Virginia who needed an intern at his church, and after two or three visits, the church voted to hire me. In almost a week's time, I booked a cruise, stocked a storage building, set a wedding date, planned a wedding, made many phone calls, and got married overlooking a lake in Bennettsville, South Carolina, on September 27, 2008. We spent our first honeymoon night in Camden, South Carolina.

The following week we drove to Florida, went on a week-long cruise, returned to South Carolina, packed both of our cars as tightly as could be, drove to Virginia, and started a *brand-new life* together. It was (and still is) a dream come true.

Marriage Tips:

1. Let it go—it's probably not worth fighting over.

2. You'll never realize how selfish you are until you get married and have to take a look at many aspects of yourself.

3. Always put your spouse first.

4. Never give up.

5. Give your spouse room—but not too much.

6. Make time to do things together; if you don't, then you won't.

7. Deal with things when they happen.

8. Kiss in the morning. Kiss at night. Kiss anytime—for no reason at all.

Love the family! Defend and promote it as the basic cell of human society; nurture it as the prime sanctuary of life. Give great care to the preparation of engaged couples and be close to young married couples, so that they will be for their children and the whole community an eloquent testimony of God's love.

--Pope John Paul II, 2001

The Picture - The Magic

Matthew and Anna (Powell) Hayes
Married December 15, 2007
Chesterfield, South Carolina

Our First Meeting... from the Viewpoint of Anna Hayes:

It was my last semester of college. I was just finishing up a day of student teaching when I received her phone call. She was calling to tell me that she had won tickets to a Mark Schultz concert and was wondering if I would be interested in attending.

I have known Mary Anne Hayes for as long as I can remember. My sisters and I would get so excited every Christmas because she would send each of us a Christmas gift that was made especially by her. She has been a great friend to my mom ever since she and my mom were in the third grade.

After agreeing to go to the concert, I called my parents to tell them the news. My mom and dad were excited that I would be getting to spend time with my mom's longtime friend, but they differed on whether or not Mary Anne might be trying to introduce me to one of her unmarried sons. The thought had never crossed my mind, so I leaned more towards my mom's point of view. I did not think of Mary Anne as my "matchmaker."

The day of the concert came and I found myself getting a bit nervous about the meeting. It had been years since I had spent one-on-one time with Mary Anne and I worried that we would run out of things to talk about. My friend dropped me off at the concert and I waited, wondering how I was to meet up with Mary Anne.

It had just started getting dark when I saw her. She was coming through the door of the building with her husband and a young guy in a red baseball cap. She introduced me to the guy, her son Matthew. I looked up and shook his hand. I was stunned at how taken aback I was by his eyes and bright smile. No one had made my heart race that way on first meeting.

Strange excitement bubbled up in my heart when Matthew ended up sitting beside me at the concert. My happiness, however, quickly turned to disappointment when he did not talk to me very much. I assumed he was seeing someone else, and had better things to do than talk to me. Mary Anne and I didn't have the same problem, however. My original fears were eased when she and I ended up not having enough time to talk about everything we wanted to discuss.

When I got back home after the concert my roommate said she could tell I had had a great time, because it was written all over my face. I mentioned meeting Matthew and about how handsome I thought he was, but that I didn't think he felt the same way. My roommate sensed something and shocked me by saying she believed he would call me the next day. I, of course, knew there was no way this would happen, and pushed the thought to the back of my mind.

My friend and I were out driving the following evening when I received the phone call. It was everything I could do not to drop the receiver when I heard Matthew's smooth voice on the other end. He was calling to say he had overheard me mention that my favorite Christian band was Third Day. He said that he happened to have tickets and backstage passes for the following weekend and was wondering if I would like to go with him. (Matthew plays the keyboard in the Christian band, Overflow.) Not yet certain if this was a date, but still excited about the opportunity, I wholeheartedly agreed to the outing.

The Proposal... from the Viewpoint of Matthew Hayes:

There are a couple things to know before I can fully explain our engagement story. The first is that while Anna was in college when we first began to date, her close proximity did not last. After graduation she moved to Georgia, a full two-and-a-half to three hours away in travel time. This was the case for over a full year of our dating relationship.

Valentine's Day was fast approaching and while I was going to be out of town playing a concert on Valentine's Day, Anna and I had arranged for her to come visit and stay at my parents' house the weekend prior to this holiday. While I am not undermining the romantic side of Valentine's Day, there was another, more practical reason for my timing. My beautiful wife is a schoolteacher and as such agrees to a yearly contract to return or not return to her school each year. Around this time of year, for those who don't know, teachers receive a form asking whether they intend to return the following school year. Knowing full well that I did not want to wait another full year to be with her, I had to act fast so that she would be able to make plans to come back to South Carolina.

Now, early on in our relationship both of us were confused as to whether we were on "dates" or not. This confusion lasted for several outings before it became clear to both of us that we were indeed going on *dates*. One of our first dates, that we both understood was a date, was riding around Clemson University and the surrounding towns taking pictures. After we had exhausted a couple of disposable cameras, we took the film to be developed at a one-hour photo, picked out albums for each other, went back to the car and spent some time arranging the photos (we had double prints made so we would each have an album to take home) for the other's album.

A friend had advised me to make sure whatever you do as a proposal is personal to you and your significant other, so I decided this would be the perfect way to propose—taking something we had shared while adding a special touch. After all, with us celebrating Valentine's Day, she would surely just assume it was nothing more than that.

On February 9, Anna got into town and though she was running a bit behind her planned arrival time, this was perfectly all right with me as I was busy making sure everything was just right. Our weekend plans, as far as Anna knew, were just to celebrate Valentine's Day.

When she arrived I met her with a blindfold. I proceeded to cover her eyes after I placed her in the passenger seat of my car. From there I drove over to Clemson University's campus, which is only a couple of stoplights from my parents' house. Once the car had come to a stop, I removed her blindfold. I had disposable cameras in hand for us to jump out and take pictures of each other around Clemson's football stadium and basketball coliseum. We continued around town to various places of interest with fun and sometimes silly pictures as keepsakes. When it was beginning to get dark and we wrapped up a film roll, we headed off to Wal-Mart to the one-hour photo processing department.

We ate something and returned to Wal-Mart impatiently awaiting our photos. Having already picked out our albums for each other, we were off to place the photos in the albums. However, instead of just sitting in the car to do this, I drove to a lighted park with a rustic fireplace and picnic tables. Separating ourselves at each end of the shelter, we carefully arranged the pictures for each other.

Now earlier in the day, my friend's father, a professional photographer, had taken a couple of pictures of the ring I intended to give to Anna. I took these pictures and put them in my car inside of my coat pocket. When I had gotten out of the car at the park, I had taken the pictures and tucked them in my album for her along with the Wal-Mart pictures.

When we separated under the shelter, I was able to place pictures of the ring in significant places in the album. I arranged the ring pictures on facing pages so as she went through the album, she would not be able to overlook what I wanted her to see so badly. I hurriedly finished, having been so anxious all night, ready for her to share in this excitement with me. I was so relieved that I did not have to hold this back much longer. It had been killing me today and all week to sneak about with this plan.Earlier in the week, with the help of Anna's sister, Becca, I had been able to find out when their parents would be at home together. With this knowledge, I had driven almost four hours each way to ask in person for their daughter's hand in marriage. We had all managed to keep a secret from my soon-to-be fiancée.

Anna, being the wonderful little perfectionist she is, was taking her time, making sure that each picture was in its precise spot. I, however, was getting quite impatient, ready for her to see this ring that was burning a hole in my pocket.

When I was finally able to persuade Anna that whatever she had already done was good, I sat down beside her and urged her to look at the way I had arranged the pictures for her. She agreed, opened her book, and proceeded to look carefully at each picture on every page. Then it happened. She turned to the pages with a picture of the ring on both sides. As she looked up at me, puzzled, I turned from beside her toward her. Dropping to one knee, pulling out the ring, I asked her to marry me. She didn't answer from being in a state of shock, I believe. I hugged her and told her that it was okay, that her parents had said it would be okay. At this point, hearing that her parents had given approval, she began to cry, not quite believing this to be reality.

I walked her to the car and drove her back to my parents' house, where she was able to recall every detail for them. Then the phone calls began, the call to her parents, to her sisters, to her college roommate who had "been right." I don't think I was able to see very much of her that weekend one on one and that was okay with me. Judging from her excitement, I had shown my love for her and it brought her much happiness. That meant much more to me.

We were married December 15, 2007, in Chesterfield, South Carolina, surrounded by special friends and loving family. Our mothers had been best friends as teenagers and here we were best friends as husband and wife.

Marriage Tips:

1. When a heated battle begins to brew and you find yourself starting to lose control, stop the discussion right away. Go to a different room away from your spouse. When you both have had time to calm down and gain some clarity, come back together and discuss the problem. *"A fool gives full vent to his anger, but a wise man keeps himself under control." (Proverbs 29:11)*

2. Set aside time every day to read scripture and pray with your spouse. *"Therefore pray for each other so that you may be healed. The prayer of a righteous man is powerful and effective." (James 5:20)*

3. Do not spend your time waiting for God to fix your spouse's issues, and forget the Lord's work in your own life. *"Why do you look at the speck of saw dust in your brother's eye and pay no attention to the plank in your own eye?" (Luke 6:41)*

4. Don't forget the small things. Be sure and remember to continually "date" your spouse. A little note left where he or she will find it or even flowers picked along the road can go a long way in encouraging your spouse. *"Let us not give up meeting together, as some are in the habit of doing, but let us encourage one another--all the more as you see the day approaching." (Hebrews 10:25)*

5. Laugh at yourselves often.

    "But may the righteous be glad and rejoice before God; may they be happy and joyful." *(Psalms 68:3)*

The happy state of Matrimony is, undoubtedly, the surest and most lasting foundations of comfort and love....the cause of all good Order of the World, and what alone preserves it from the Utmost Confusion....

> --Benjamin Franklin, Rules and Maxims for Promoting Matrimonial Happiness, 1730

The Twist, the Shag Era

Jim and Lynn Hicks
June 22, 1968
Spartanburg, South Carolina

I first met Jimmy when he began dating one of my friends. Most of my friends had grown up in Spartanburg, but Jimmy had only lived there since the eighth grade. My friends and I were sophomores and he was a high school junior when I got to know him.

Jimmy and his sister began having their friends visit from his former hometown. Since we lived on the same street, we all started getting together, hanging out, having dance parties (the Twist, the Shag, etc.). By March of 1962 I had met and begun dating one of Jimmy's former hometown friends.

As the high school years came to an end, Jimmy and I went off to different colleges but always kept in touch through letters and phone calls. We saw each other when we were home from college and had the occasional friendly date, as our sweethearts were in other towns.

We eventually broke up with our high school sweethearts and at different times "cried on each others' shoulders" for solace. As we turned to each other more and more, we became more connected and Jimmy asked me to marry him. We became engaged on August 19, 1967.

It was a year of excitement and "busyness" as I had my first job and was planning a wedding. Jimmy was studying hard in his second year of veterinary medicine at the University of Georgia.

Our wedding was on June 22, 1968. It was a typical Southern wedding, surrounded by family and friends, held at dusk at my beloved First Baptist Church of Spartanburg. We arrived at our hotel in Charlotte, North Carolina. I did not think we would ever get there. I was extremely tired from the events of the previous week and our wedding. We were both totally exhausted. The next morning was an early one as we had a very long drive to reach our honeymoon destination in Ocracoke Island, North Carolina. I have to admit there was not very much to do on the island but fish, sleep, eat, fish, and fish some more. I was glad when it was time to travel to Jimmy's best friend's wedding in Jefferson City, Tennessee. Jimmy was a groomsman in Pat's wedding as Pat had been in ours the week before. Oh, and did I mention that Pat was my old boyfriend?

The festivities of that weekend were enjoyable, also, but then it was time to return home to Spartanburg, pack our things, and head to Athens, Georgia, where our life together really began.

Jimmy completed his last two years of veterinary school. I taught in a local preschool and shelved books at the University of Georgia library. It was fun to become a part of a group of rising professionals and all the partying that goes on in a professional fraternity. One particular highlight was when we won the first-place prize for our costumes at the annual fraternity Hobo Ball. Our prize was a five-dollar gift certificate for two steak dinners. This was a treat for a struggling veterinary student and his bride who were used to soup and hot dogs.

The following year our first baby was on her way, and she was six months old when her daddy graduated from veterinary school. We left Athens in 1970. Jimmy's Army training at Fort Sam Houston in San Antonio, Texas, was starting. After six weeks Missie, our daughter, and I went back to Spartanburg and Jimmy went to his next training station in Chicago, Illinois, for eight weeks.

Our second baby, little Jim, was born March 26, 1971, at Fort Benning, Georgia. Jimmy found out in January that he would be leaving for Korea in June, but did not tell me until we brought the baby home from the hospital. I was understandably upset but thankful it was not to Viet Nam.

Then we headed back to Spartanburg where the children and I rented a duplex and I stayed busy taking care of them, sending care packages to Jimmy, and waiting every day for his letters to come. After his return from Korea, Jimmy and I had our third child, Rob. Our lives took many courses. We finally settled in Fernandina Beach, Florida.

The one thing that has always sustained us as a couple is that Jimmy and I never forgot the friendship bond we had developed earlier. There is a loyalty in deep friendship that cannot be broken. No matter what affected our marriage, the friendship bond could not be diminished. Both of us had a "stick-to-it-ness" and the love of God. Bringing up our children together was (and has been) more important to us than anything else.

When times would get rough, we were blessed to find a third party who could help and that made all the difference. Our goal was to remain an intact family. When we were young, we were not as quick to forgive one another but we never let go of our love, friendship, and commitment to each other. That staying power helped us win out. It made love sweeter, more pure, and more eternal. (It sometimes takes twenty to twenty-five years together to realize all of this. Then you do not want the marriage to ever end.)

We made sure that we did a lot of enjoyable things (activities, trips, etc.) together as a family. We believed and now know that this was the glue that held us and our family together.

The happiness now is enjoying our children and grandchildren. It is sweeter knowing that we have a marriage that has lasted and will continue in God's home for eternity.

Marriage Tips:

1. Love God.

2. Have many Christian friends.

3. Attend church and take your family with you.

4. Pray.

5. Be kind.

6. Encourage laughter, joy, and humility together.

7. Go to God and trust Him.

8. Have loyalty and commitment to one another.

9. Forgive.

10. Read and study to further spiritual growth.

When there is love in a marriage, there is harmony in the home; when there is harmony in the home, there is contentment in the community; when there is contentment in the community, there is prosperity in the nation; when there is prosperity in the nation, there is peace in the world.

-- Chinese proverb

Six Months Honeymoon

Cyril and Mary Jo Higgs
Married October 28, 1992
Stratford-upon-Avon
Warwickshire, England

My youngest daughter, Cathy, was engaged. The date had been set and the invitations sent. I met the groom's family and they immediately began to tell me about their friend who was coming from England. I had been divorced for years and I felt they were trying to play matchmaker. They were and it worked.

Cyril and his daughter, Debbie, arrived in the morning, and that night Cathy and I were invited to meet them and have dinner. The dinner went well, everyone talked and laughed, and I felt very comfortable. After dinner everyone disappeared while Cyril and I were talking in the kitchen. He began to tell me about his recent trip to Spain—he had a new car and while racing a Porsche through France at a hundred miles per hour (they were the only two cars on the road, according to Cyril), Cyril got pulled over and was fined a substantial amount. His reasoning was that his car had English plates and the Porsche had French plates—so, the Frenchman did not get stopped. I should have known then how fast he plays.

The next day he called me at work and invited me to dinner, but my oldest daughter and family were coming in for the wedding and I felt I should meet them. We arranged to meet at Leo's, a fine Italian restaurant in Macon, Georgia. Cathy, Carla, Jim and I came from Warner Robins, and John, Debbie and Cyril, from Dublin. When everyone arrived, after quick introductions, Cyril slipped John a hundred dollars and told them to get pizza some place else and pick us up at midnight. They gladly took the money and left.

We were seated at an enclosed booth with candlelight—very romantic—for four hours. The food was delicious and the conversation never stopped … it was like Lady and the Tramp (☺) except we had fish instead of spaghetti.

Cyril had lost his wife to cancer six months earlier after a long, happy marriage and was lonely. I was divorced and lonely. Cyril had told his friends he wanted to meet a Christian lady and I had been asking God to send me a good, Christian man. I just had not expected him to be from across the pond. The more we talked, the more we realized how compatible we were. I asked if he would be my escort for the wedding. He accepted and he has been escorting me ever since.

The day after the wedding, Cyril and I disappeared—or so the family thought. We went to the Museum of Aviation in Warner Robins and from there to the Macon Mall—he liked to shop back then. We had lunch at Ruby Tuesday's. When we arrived at my mother's house that evening, all the family was there and wanted a full account of our whereabouts.

The next day Cyril and Debbie left to join the newlyweds and John's family in St. Thomas (that's another story). He invited me to join them, but I had to work. He called every night while there. About the fifth or sixth night he asked me to marry him. I do not remember what I said but it must have been "yes." I remember walking out of the bedroom into the living room and telling my mother, aunt, and cousin that Cyril had asked me to marry him. We were all in shock.

Cyril and Debbie returned, with Debbie, going to Dublin, and Cyril, going to Warner Robins. When he left two days later for England, he left a ring on my finger. I took him to the airport. He called every morning before I left for work and every evening after I returned from work. After a couple of weeks, he said, "These phone calls are costing me a lot of money. Quit that job, come to England and marry me." That very day I gave my notice at work. I later said to him, "If you don't mean it, you had better say it to me." Within two weeks I had indeed quit my job, packed my bags and left for England.

My cousin took me to the Atlanta Airport and Cyril met me at Heathrow Airport in England. We traveled from there to Stratford-upon-Avon, Cyril's home, stopping for lunch at Shipton-on-Stour. I had never been to England and I immediately fell in love with the country, just as I had the Englishman. We were married a week later, Wednesday, October 28, 1992, at 10 a.m., at the Stratford Registry Office. The wedding lunch was held at the King's Head Inn, Aston Canlow, in the same room where William Shakespeare's parents held their wedding breakfast. The autumn leaves were red and gold and looked like a carpet laid for us as we walked through the parking lot into the inn. All of Cyril's children were there, along with two sisters and numerous friends. A good time was had by all.

Cyril's pastor (Ray Heritage) was away when we married but upon his return, he performed a beautiful Christian marriage ceremony. Three elderly ladies of the church had made floral arrangements and refreshments, and were wearing big smiles. We were the only ones there—six of us, but it was a beautiful, meaningful ceremony. We stayed, talking with Ray for a long time. I guess that was our counseling. He became my good friend, too, as well as Cyril's, and he visited us often.

The first trip we took to Spain was in mid-November. Cyril had a large house there and needed to take care of business. We ate, enjoyed the warm sun, visited ruins and took care of business. On our return he wanted to take me to Andorra in the Pyrenees Mountains. We drove to Andorra, stayed at a lovely hotel, shopped, and of course, ate, ate, ate—I had already gained four pounds eating my way across Europe.

We left Andorra driving down the other side of France but as we left, it started to snow. A couple of hours later we found ourselves slipping and sliding—almost into a house on the side of the mountain. Nice folks came out, helped right the car, and told us there was a ski resort/hotel just down the road and we should stop there. We did—for three days. I loved it! We watched the skiers coming down the mountain, read and ate.

On the third day Cyril could not be still another hour. He announced that he was going for tire chains and we were leaving. I watched as he dug the completely covered car out of the snow by hand. Chains were put on and we left the next morning. It was a beautiful day but the mountain roads were icy and like hairpins. I screamed out more than once and was surprised to find after stopping, no holes in the floorboard. I had been braking along with Cyril all down the mountain. At one point ahead of us was a stalled car on the bend. Cyril had to go around on the outside with nothing but air on the right. God was surely with us.

When we arrived at the bottom at a little village in France, we stopped and gave thanks and I kissed the flat ground. We also wanted lunch but in Europe lunch is over by 2 p.m. and every restaurant closes until evening. We found a bar with a toilet. The toilet was a hole in the floor with the mountain stream running underneath and was for both men and women. This Georgia girl had never seen such a thing but I did not let it stop me.

We arrived back in England to find that Cyril's grandson, Jesse, had been born and his granddaughter, Charlie, was due any day. Next we traveled to Holland to spend Thanksgiving with my sister and family and they joined us, along with my mother and brother, in England just after Christmas.

In February we took a wonderful cruise down the Nile River from Luxor to Aswan, Egypt, and back. Cyril calls that trip our honeymoon, but I think the whole six months we lived in England was a honeymoon. I had seen and gone places I never dreamed I'd go and all with the good, Christian man God had sent me.

Cyril and I are still traveling. We have children and grandchildren on three continents; Australia, Europe, and North America. Cyril has three sons (Andrew, Adrian, and David), one daughter (Debbie) and eight grandchildren. I have one son (Neil) and one daughter (Carla) and three grandchildren. All our children have met and enjoy our combined families.

We lost Cathy in 1998 but continue to thank God for her part in bringing us together. She remains in our hearts and memories.

Marriage Tips:

1. God, family, church: keep that order.
2. Patience: Cyril is better at this than I am, but I keep trying.
3. Acceptance: Try not to change in the other what attracted you in the first place.
4. Understanding: They say we speak the same language but he's still saying "eh" and I'm still saying "huh."
5. Laugh: Laugh a lot!!
6. Pray: Pray in all the between times. God does answer prayers; we are perfect examples.

Dear Abby: Some months ago, you printed a letter from a reader who was disturbed that the spark was gone from her marriage. I asked my husband whether the spark is gone from our 18-year marriage. His response: "A spark lasts only a second. It lights the fire. When the flame burns down, we are left with the hottest part of the fire, the embers, which burn the longest and keep the fire alive."

-- Betty in Cape May, New Jersey

Fifty-Four Extraordinary Years and More

Dan and Anne Kirby
Married October 1, 1955
Jacksonville, Florida

It was a cool February evening in 1955 when the Minor-Kirby relationship began. My mother, already widowed, and I lived in our family home on the north side of Jacksonville, Florida. I had purchased a beautiful goldenrod yellow, 1954 Ford convertible a few months earlier. We were frequent visitors to Fernandina Beach, as my parents owned property there.

This particular evening I had gone to pick up my cousin who stayed with us during the week, as she had to work late. Just as we arrived at home, a beautiful new coral and gray Chevrolet rounded the corner. There to our surprise were two young men—one was a mutual friend and the other was none other than Dan Kirby, whom we did not know. The two young men had been "riding around" in Dan's brand-new car. The mutual friend had told him that he knew a girl he would like to introduce to him. So here I was.

We all rode around a little in Dan's new car and became acquainted. After the ride, we returned to my home and said our goodbyes. It was a month later before I saw him again.

It was mid-March and two of my teenage cousins and I had decided to go to Fernandina Beach for the weekend. Their grandmother, my aunt, had a beach house on South Fletcher Avenue, so we thought we would stay over the weekend. The only catch was that the house had been winterized—water cut off. As we sat at Main Beach contemplating the situation, who should come driving up but Dan. He saw the yellow Ford convertible with three girls inside and stopped. He was our knight in shining armor. He got us some jugs of water from his uncle's house, and he escorted us back to our house. He had to go to work that night at midnight at Rayonier Mill. He asked if he could come and see us the next day and I, of course, said yes. After that day he came every chance he had to Jacksonville to see me.

I found myself going to Fernandina every chance I had, staying in my aunt's house with my cousins.

One night in June as Dan and I were sitting at Main Beach looking at the ocean, he said, "When are we going to get married?" and my reply was, "Not before February."

We were married October 1, 1955, at 5 p.m. at the First Presbyterian Church in Jacksonville, by Dr. Jack G. Hand. There were three attendants to the bride and three groomsmen. We had a beautiful reception at the home of my favorite cousin, the mother of the teenagers who were often with me on our trips to Fernandina Beach.

Our honeymoon was a trip to Fontana Village in the mountains of North Carolina. At the time I had never been to the mountains before. It was breathtakingly beautiful. We have tried to return to the mountains during that time every year since 1955 when at all possible.

My mother, better known as Nana, lived with us our entire married life with the exception of two years. It was a great experience for us as well as for our son and daughter. Nana died in 1994 at the age of ninety-eight. We sold our home in Jacksonville and moved to Fernandina in 1973. We converted our beach house into our present home. I retired from my job in Jacksonville in 1974 and soon became employed in Fernandina in the Nassau County Tax Collector's office where I stayed until 2003. Dan retired from Rayonier Mill in 1996 after forty-three years.

Dan and I have had a wonderful life together. We have been married fifty-four extraordinary years.

Marriage Tips:

1. Always respect each other's opinions.

2. Never go to sleep at night irritated with one another.

3. Don't argue.

4. Manage finances together.

5. Be involved in a church family.

Ultimately, the bond of all companionship whether in marriage or in friendship, is conversation.

-- *Oscar Wilde*

Dating My Best Friend?
That Would Be Weird!

Jonathan and Rachel (Renfrow) Lawrence
Married June 7, 2008
Gastonia, North Carolina

After spending the summer before my sophomore year in Uganda, Africa, I returned to Columbia International University a week early to help out with new student orientation. I was responsible for leading a group of students around from activity to activity and for making sure they felt welcome. One afternoon, we were supposed to be going on and helping with a scavenger hunt, but the scheduling didn't quite work out. I was told to stall and "just keep them talking," not an easy task with a group full of nervous freshmen who have just met one another. As the time stretched on, it got more and more awkward. I was grasping for any conversation starter. "So … anyone have any … pets?"

I don't know if he felt sorry for me or just really loved his dog that much, but one guy piped up and started talking about his black poodle named Wickett. The ice was broken, and everyone started to relax. I knew I'd be forever grateful to this kid. I did not know I'd just met my best friend.

Jonathan and I got to know each other that fall, mostly because he liked a girl on my hall at the time. We hung out occasionally and talked about random things like our favorite books and poems. In the spring, our friendship really took off. Together we helped to organize an event to raise awareness for the war in Uganda. We went on trips to Wal-Mart and Waffle House, walked around campus, and confided in one another about the people we liked and our struggles with our calls to missions. I never once thought about Jonathan romantically. In fact, when someone once asked if we were dating, I laughed in her face and told her, "Oh, no. That'd be weird."

Over the summer, we kept in touch on the phone and internet; he was one of the people I looked most forward to seeing when school started back. He'd also decided over the break to go on a team with me and a few other students to Uganda during the New Year's holidays.

We spent more and more time together at the beginning of the new semester and had so much fun. Jonathan became like a brother to me, listening to me cry about boys, threatening to beat up people who hurt my feelings, and making me laugh when I was sad. He also kept me updated on the progress he was making with a girl he liked and was talking to long distance.

One night, he called to say he'd just been on the phone with this particular girl and wanted to talk to me about it. He came over and told me that she'd let him know that she was interested in a relationship. I was so excited for him … but also really upset. I did not tell him this at the time, but it was bothering me that I had mixed emotions. These emotions tortured me for about a week. I called my mom to talk it over.

"I think it's like when Stephen (my brother) got married and I was jealous because I knew things wouldn't be the same," I explained to her.

"Or maybe you like him," she said.

"No, I don't *like* him in that way." I must have repeated that statement a hundred times during that phone conversation. I think I said it as much for me as for my mom. "I don't feel like I do when I like someone. It's not like that." Then she told me something very important.

"Rachel, there does not always have to be fireworks. I'd rather you end up with your best friend than just someone you feel fireworks around." She had a good point, but I didn't *like* him. I let her know that a few more times before we got off the phone.

After we talked, I thought about it some more and was finally coming to terms with the fact that things were changing and I needed to be happy for my friend. Then the night came when everything would change.

Jonathan and I were just hanging out as usual. We'd played capture the flag and gone to a bonfire on campus earlier that night. I don't remember what we were talking about, but he made reference to something we should do together when we grew up. Not realizing how harsh it might sound to someone who had not been thinking about and dealing with the future of our friendship over the past week, I said, "Jonathan, we probably won't even know each other in five years."

"What? That's terrible," he reacted. "You don't want to be friends in five years?"

"It's not that," I said. "I just don't think your girlfriend or wife will be cool with you coming and hanging out with me this often."

"Oh, I hadn't thought about that. I'm not okay with that."

"Well, that's how it's going to be."

"No. We'll figure something out. I'm not sure what, but it will be okay."

Things were very different after that night. We started talking more and more about the future and the direction each of us thought we would go after school. It became clear that we either needed to pursue marriage or part ways at this point. It wouldn't work for us to be this close anymore and not be together forever. By now, I knew that I liked him (why are moms always right?), but things were out of my hands. Plus, there was another girl involved still.

Jonathan did a lot of praying and talking to his youth pastor back home. About a week later (on Columbus Day) while we were studying, he said we needed to talk. He took me outside and told me that he liked me. He was going to break things off with the other girl and wanted to pursue me … "with the intention of marrying you," he said. I was very happy. The fireworks had come.

We went to Uganda over New Year's, and I saw him fall in love with the kids that meant so much to me. We talked a lot more about the future on that trip. He bought a white ring from the market there and asked my parents for permission to marry me the night we flew home. He asked me a few days later. (I wore that African ring for several months before we went shopping for a diamond; it's one of my most treasured possessions.)

We were engaged for almost a year and a half and finally got married on June 7, 2008, at my home church in Gastonia, North Carolina. We honeymooned in Myrtle Beach, South Carolina, and flew to Japan a few days later to spend the summer working with missionaries there. It was an amazing way to start our lives together.

We settled in Columbia, South Carolina, after that. The fireworks are definitely still there, but more than anything, I'm thankful to be married to my best friend. Many of our weekends are spent building forts in our living room, eating pizza, and watching movies. I look forward to many more adventures and good times together.

Marriage Tips:

1. Love is a choice, not just a feeling. Choose to love your spouse even on days when you don't feel fireworks.

2. The whole point of grace is that it is undeserved. Show grace to your spouse like Christ has shown it to you.

3. Be best friends with your spouse; life is much more fun that way.

4. Deal with problems and disagreements as soon as they arise; grudges are not fun. Besides, you'll have to deal with them eventually, so go ahead, get them out of the way and have fun again.

5. Have lots of traditions (even silly ones); it keeps you close even when life gets crazy.

6. Make being the best spouse you can, your number one job, before your other jobs (or your schoolwork, etc.)

7. Letting God make you into the man and woman He wants you to be is the best thing you can ever do for your spouse.

Marriage, ultimately, is the practice of becoming passionate friends.

-- Harville Hendrix

A Red Bow on Gable's Collar

Roger and Dina (Dobrosky) Martin
Married June 26, 2004
Fernandina Beach, Florida

Roger and I met in May of 2002 at the Women's Community Bible Study on Amelia Island, Florida. Roger, who had just moved to the island eight months earlier, was asked to give the opening devotion about using your time wisely with God. Obviously, the audience was all women and his opening line was, "How lucky am I, speaking to this room of lovely ladies and I'm a single guy." Instead of the usual laughs he had gotten before, it seemed as though every eye in the room turned to me. I, too, was single, born and raised on Amelia Island in Fernandina Beach, and I owned a children's toy store. Needless to say, not many single men frequented my shop. Several women had been in the "matchmaking" business where the two of us were concerned, and we were quickly introduced after his talk. We found that we had a common interest in getting a Teen Community Bible Study *started* on the island.

Our initial encounter was brief but later that evening I was at a restaurant with friends, listening to live music. Roger and a friend walked in and were not able to find a table because it was extremely crowded. As they were about to leave, the table next to us cleared. I motioned for them to join our group. Roger sat next to me and we ended up talking all evening and learned that we not only had God and Teen CBS in common but many other things as well. I told my visiting college roommate, who was with me that night, that I had just met the guy I was going to marry. I would later learn that Roger called his sister that same evening and told her that he had just met the girl he was going to marry.

Our friendship soon developed into something more. After dating for several months we both could see that we were falling in love and began talking about our future together. While I was away on a market buying trip for my store in October of 2003, Roger had planned to propose to me on his birthday. He had already talked to my parents and had their blessing. Unfortunately, I was delayed in my return as we were supposed to meet at my house. He was watching my dog, Gable, and after a walk they came home and both fell asleep on my couch. I later learned that the engagement ring was in his pocket the whole time.

It took him another whole month to find the perfect time to propose. My parents were worried that he had gotten cold feet. I kept wondering why my parents were so interested in whether I had talked to Roger each day or not.

On November 22, Roger planned to reenact our first date. We traveled to Jacksonville, ate at the same restaurant, walked along the river walk and then returned to my house. When we got to my house, Roger volunteered to take Gable for a quick walk. Gable was my baby and was very attached to me. I had always joked with Roger that if Gable didn't like him, he was out. How fitting that when Roger and Gable returned from their walk, the engagement ring was tied to Gable's collar. I quickly noticed the sparkle hanging from a red bow. In my excitement I nearly broke Gable's neck trying to get to the ring. Roger said that Gable had obviously given us his blessing, too, and then he got down on one knee and asked me to marry him. I couldn't say *"yes"* fast enough.

Roger was naïve about what would happen next. He thought his job was done and now I could plan the wedding. As word quickly spread across the island, visitors, phone calls and invitations to friends' homes soon filled our Sunday afternoons, which he thought were going to be spent relaxing and watching NFL games. The planning began and the date was set for June 26, 2004. We knew the wedding ceremony was going to be very special for both of us. It was in the same church (St. Michael's Catholic Church) where my parents, William and Carolyn Dobrosky, and godparents, Everett and Jackie Howard, got married nearly fifty years before.

Roger had worked at First Presbyterian Church and at our initial meeting with Father Brian, he asked if there was some way that his pastor could participate in the wedding service. Father Brian chuckled and said, "I love a man who brings his own pastor to his wedding," and was extremely gracious and said he admired Rev. Conrad Sharps and would be delighted to let him participate and even do the Homily. After our meeting with Father Brian we went straight to First Presbyterian Church to speak with Conrad about the ceremony. As Roger's pastor, former boss and one of his best friends, he was excited to be able to participate in the ceremony and honored to do the Homily. My godparents had always played an important part in my life and we wanted them to be included in the ceremony as well. We asked them to bring forth the rings and they did so with tears of joy.

Our special day finally came. After the vows were said, the rings exchanged, and our first married kiss, we walked down the aisle. All of my friends recognized the song, "Dancing Queen" by Abba, mixed into our traditional recessional song by our very talented organist. We were taken from the ceremony by horse and buggy to our reception at a well-known restaurant, Brett's Waterway Café, overlooking the Amelia River. We thoroughly enjoyed our time with friends and family at the reception. Many of Roger's friends were looking for a car to decorate but no one knew of our plan to leave the reception by boat. When the time came for us to part, our friends and family walked down with us on the docks to send us off with white, pink and brown balloons.

Since June is a busy time for both of our businesses, we were unable to get away for a full honeymoon. We enjoyed several days in Ponte Vedra, playing golf, getting massages and just relaxing. In September we took our delayed honeymoon to San Francisco and Napa Valley, California. We spent a week exploring the West Coast, including seeing a San Francisco Giants baseball game, visiting the aquarium at Monterrey and driving along the Pacific Coast Highway to the Redwood Forest. After taking many pictures, including us riding bikes over the Golden Gate Bridge, viewing Alcatraz, and visiting the beautiful vineyards of Napa Valley, our digital camera on the last day of our trip reformatted the disk and we lost all of our pictures. Fortunately, Roger and I have a great sense of humor and anytime someone mentions San Francisco, we laugh with each other and say that we need to get out our honeymoon album and look at our wonderful pictures.

Roger and I both agree that we are extremely blessed to have my parents in our lives. They are an inspiration to us as they have been married over fifty years now. Roger's parents both passed away when he was young and my parents lost their oldest son when he was nineteen. All of us feel as though God returned to Roger, new parents, and to my parents, a new son. In addition, my parents serve as wonderful Christian role models and we both genuinely enjoy spending family time together.

We have also been blessed by God to have a precious daughter, Caroline, who was born in December of 2006. She is a joy to all of us and we treasure the time we spend together as a family.

Marriage Tips:

1. This June (2009) we will be celebrating our fifth wedding anniversary. Putting God first in our marriage is the first step that has made us successful.

2. We both love each other but realize that our love for one another and for God is secondary to the love He has for us.

3. We try to surround ourselves with Christian fellowship.

4. Communication is also another important element in being happy together. The ability to share anything and everything with each other helps in developing and maturing our relationship.

5. Laughter has always been a part of our lives—our ability to laugh with one another and often at ourselves. That reminds me of when I was preparing dinner for Roger one night soon after our wedding and suggested I make stir-fry like I did when we were dating. Roger quickly informed me that he did not like stir-fry. I was shocked and said that he ate it when we were dating. He said the key word in that sentence was "dating." We both began to laugh and to this day I have not made stir-fry but will suggest it to get a good laugh.

6. Finally, supporting one another in our businesses and hobbies allows us to share with each other good times and bad.

The goal in marriage is not to think alike, but to think together.

-- Robert C. Dodds

A Match Made In T-Ball Heaven

Ben and Jocelyn (Rogers) Renfrow
Married June 5, 1999
Dillon, South Carolina

A Christian song artist, Steven Curtis Chapman, wrote: "I will be an Honest Heart you can depend on; I will be a Faithful Friend."

From an early age God began merging our paths. I had met a new friend. She played left field, a position she chose to play on our Kiwanis t-ball team so that while her teammates and I were busy trying to remember where the coach had told us to stand, she could gather all of the spring flowers that were blooming out near the outfield fence. She understood that this was just a silly old sport and not worth taking too seriously. Something about her caught my eye.

Several years later my family left a small, local church in Kemper, South Carolina, to attend First Baptist Church, in the big town of Dillon, South Carolina. While many things were new and different, my old teammate was there. She was the star of the youth group. Beautiful, confident … and she always played the leading role in our church plays. She understood what was important and became a good friend. Even when my beard fell off in front of hundreds of audience members during a production of the Christmas cantata, she remained a faithful and loyal friend.

During the summer after our seventh-grade year, Jocelyn was really growing into a responsible Christian leader in the community. She applied for and was given a position to work at Camp Pine Hill, a popular Christian camp in South Carolina. I decided to work there, as well, on the work crew. We had both been there many times as campers. It was no mistake that God brought us to this camp together. She was again a star. She sang and did skits and impressed everyone with spiritual maturity. Several of my sisters insisted that she would be a good catch. I knew it, but the timing was not quite right (that reads … I was too scared to let my friend know that I was falling for her). I could not keep my eyes off of her and I watched her from a distance … Unfortunately, so did the rest of the work crew.

Another member of the crew beat me to the proverbial "punch." He asked her to "go with him." She said yes. Fortunately for me he was from out of state. This was later understood to be part of God's plan. I put up the typical tough guy "wall." My heart was broken and I let her know it. After the "other guy" went back home, I knew that I better make my move before I lost her again. I had fallen in love at the age of thirteen, with my former teammate and loyal friend.

We started dating (i.e., we talked on the telephone and she wore my football jerseys). It was not long until God started working even more in our lives, testing us. There was distance; we went to different high schools and had different friends. I also fell in love with sports and made it my idol. She had her priorities in order and focused on school and dance. We drifted in and out of a typical high school relationship. We talked about marriage and families and living happily ever after. But God was building a friendship that encountered many trivial bumps and bruises. Regardless, we were friends and even at our worst had mutual respect and friendship for one another.

We went off to different colleges. We broke up, as God would see it. We did our own things for over a year. We grew up and matured. On her birthday in 1996, our sophomore year, I called her to wish her well. There was a spark! She called me back a few weeks later. I went to see her. I asked my high school sweetheart to go to the beach with my family for a November getaway. She went and underneath a walkway at Ocean Isle Beach, we decided to give it one more go and if it was meant to be, God would renew the love we once thought we had.

We prayed and asked God to show if we were meant to be together. He did and it swept us both off of our feet. We had never experienced love like this, and very soon we both knew that God had been developing this relationship even before we had any idea what his plan was for our lives.

I went out and purchased a ring during my junior year of college. The jewelry store was so patient and allowed me to pay what I could, when I could. I knew she would like it, as we had looked around together. It was small and not very expensive but I could not tell anyone what I was going to do. I worked three work-study jobs and used every penny I made to pay off the ring. (I saved every penny I had left *after* taking many trips from Wofford College to Clemson University. Luckily gas was cheap at the time, only sixty-nine cents a gallon. I could drive that route in my sleep and I think I did a few times.)

I continued to save money. I cleaned up a baseball field. After class but before baseball practice I would work as a runner at a local law firm. I then worked in the computer lab as a security guard without a gun. Those hours in the computer lab were long and hard (10 p.m. until 2 a.m., for three or four nights a week) but the money was good. I finally paid off the ring.

I then told everyone I had a bad cavity and had to travel home to see my dentist. I called her dad and asked for his blessing. We met at Hardee's. He was great and gave his blessing so long as we promised not to marry on a Clemson University football weekend. I reluctantly approached my dad as well, and philosophically told him "I know I am only twenty-one years old, but I am certain she is the one God has for me." He very calmly looked me in the eye and said "Son, I do not think you are too young. I was married and had four kids before I was your age." I was relieved to have the necessary blessings!

We were married a few weeks after college graduation. We went to Jamaica for our honeymoon. We then took a one-year extended honeymoon to Denver, Colorado. Our relationship grew and we became the best of friends, dependent upon each other for just about everything.

We have now been married almost ten years, have three wonderful children, and our friendship continues to grow. Since our sophomore year in college neither of us has ever had any doubt that we were meant to be together. We are not perfect and we continue to work at this great God-ordained institution of marriage. But as that Christian artist eloquently wrote (that song was part of our wedding), we are faithful friends and depend on each other through good times and bad.

The journey continues ...

Marriage Tips:
Hers:

1. Figure out your mate's love language and nurture that.

2. Remember, what works for your marriage may not work for others ... that is okay.

3. Women, slow down and spend time with your husband; there will always be housework to do.

4. Treasure the short moments together.

5. Always remember the gift God has given you.

His:

1. Do not go to bed mad.

2. The man should always drive the car. ☺

3. Pray together.

4. Continue to date.

5. Men ... always lower the toilet seat when finished. ☺

There is nothing nobler or more admirable than when two people who see eye to eye keep house as man and wife, confounding their enemies and delighting their friends.

Homer

Shock. Elation.
Incredulity. Thankfulness.

Jamie and Carla Renfrow
Married April 6, 1991
Lake City, South Carolina

Jamie and I met in August 1987, knew each other for three and a half years, and married in April 1991. That's the short story. But the long version has more drama, ups and downs, than you may want to know.

I graduated from Furman University in Greenville, South Carolina, in the spring of 1987 with plans to attend the University of South Carolina Law School that fall. Jamie graduated from West Point Academy in New York in 1977, served in the U.S. Army for five years, and returned to his home, Dillon County, South Carolina, where he was elected and served as Probate Judge for four years. During those four years, he decided to go to law school, and he, too, began USC Law School in the fall of 1987. We started law school in the same class, and we both graduated in December 1989, one semester early.

When law school started, Jamie and I didn't know each other. We actually met early in our first semester in the student lounge of the law school (how romantic…). When I decided definitely to begin USC Law School in the fall of 1987, a college friend of mine, Elizabeth Belcher, told me of her former Sunday School teacher, Mel Williamson, who was also slated to start in the fall of 1987. Elizabeth said the nicest things about Mel and his wife Debbie. She encouraged me to meet Mel and Debbie and to get to know them. Imagine my surprise when, during the first week or so of school, I walked into the student lounge to buy a Coke, started making small talk with two male law students sitting in the lounge, and found out that one of them was Mel Williamson. After introducing myself to Mel, he introduced me to a friend of his, Jamie Renfrow.

When Mel introduced me to Jamie, I assumed he was married just as Mel was married. Jamie looked like a "married man," so I thought he was. Over the next couple of weeks, I ran into Jamie at school, and always he was a gentleman. I saw him at a first-year law school party, in the lobby at school, and in two classes that we had together. During one of our first torts classes, I remember the professor calling on "Mr. Renfrow" to answer some questions during the class. When I heard his very Southern "yes, sir," and "no, sir," I turned to find out who was speaking. I knew the person speaking had to be from my part of the world—the Pee Dee—based on his accent. I soon found out that Mr. Renfrow was, in fact, from the Pee Dee.

One of my favorite memories happened the Friday before Labor Day. After classes that day, everyone scrambled to leave school for the long weekend. I, too, hurried to leave, but it was pouring rain. Since I lived a couple of blocks from school, I walked every day. Because of the downpour, I waited by the door, looking out the window for a break in the rain and the best chance to dash home. All of a sudden, Jamie rounded the corner, told me he had an umbrella, and ran upstairs to get it for me. I was so impressed! I kept insisting I would be okay, but he kept insisting that I should use his umbrella. I used the umbrella … and found out how kind and considerate Jamie was.

The next encounter I had with him was on a Saturday morning when several of us were to get together for a study session at Jamie's house. Mel, a friend named Joan, Jamie and I were in a study group for two classes we had together. We planned to study one Saturday morning to get a jump-start on making outlines for our classes. I showed up at Jamie's house on time (that was during my On-Time Era), but Mel and Joan weren't there. We chatted while we waited for them to come. We talked about law school, our professors, the classes, and, of course, USC football. Jamie asked if I were going to the game that night (at USC), and, because it was supposed to rain, I said, "No, I don't do ballgames in the rain." Eventually Mel and Joan each called to say they couldn't join us, so I went home prepared to study on my own the rest of the afternoon and evening.

During the afternoon the rain set in. It poured most of the afternoon, so by game time, everything and everywhere was soaked. About 7 p.m. Jamie called to ask me if I wanted to have dinner with him, since he had decided not to go to the game because of the rain (Imagine that!?!). I accepted his invitation, and we went to Yesterdays for dinner where I was thoroughly enthralled by Jamie's gentlemanly manners, engaging conversation, and wild stories! Can you believe he told me that he was one of eleven children? He could actually name his siblings when I asked him to do so, but he couldn't give me their birthdates. *Aha*! The thought actually crossed my mind that I was out on a date with a pathological liar☺! Additionally, as we talked about our families and lives pre-law school, I found out that Jamie was ten years older than I. Immediately, I remember thinking, "Well, this is our last date … I don't date people ten years older than I am."

My "first date" with Jamie turned out to be fantastic for me. I eventually realized that he was really one of eleven children and that, though he was ten years older, he had never been married. I realized he wasn't a pathological liar and was actually a very kind soul. When Jamie took me home, he was such a gentleman and said goodbye at the door. I remember coming in from the evening feeling uplifted and refreshed. I called my mother that night to tell her about the date with Jamie. I remember telling her that he would be a very special person in my life. While I would discourage anyone from acting on "love at first sight" feelings, I do believe it can happen. And, while I wouldn't say it was love at first sight with Jamie, I knew that night that he would be significant to me.

Perhaps because of my youth (twenty-two) or because of "love," I was ready to spend lots of time with Jamie, but he took things slowly with me. Every day I saw him in the lobby before and in between classes, and I saw him in the two classes we had together. I also saw him in the library between classes where many of us studied during the day. From time to time on the weekends, we would do something together, usually dinner, a movie, a law school event, or a football game.

Additionally, I signed up to play on the first-year's female intramural basketball team. When I found out that we didn't have a coach, I told the girls on the team that I knew someone who might coach us. When I asked Jamie about coaching, he readily took the job, saying something like, "Well, it's a sacrifice for me, but somebody's got to do it!" So, for at least two more nights a week, I would usually see him at the gym where we either had practice or a game. Also, from time to time, he had friends who came to Columbia for work-related reasons. He introduced me to his friends (Rick, Kevin, and Virgie) and would invite me to join them often when they would eat dinner together. The more I was around Jamie, the more I realized how much I admired him and how important he was becoming to me. I thought the time we spent together was precious to both of us, but I soon found out that knowing how Jamie felt about me was not easy, nor did he feel about me the way I did about him.

The first clue I had that Jamie wasn't on the same page with me in this relationship was when he went to West Point for his ten-year class reunion. The reunion was sometime in the fall, so I had known Jamie for two to three months when he took the trip. One Wednesday during one of our breaks, he casually told me that he would not be at school the next two days because he was going to his reunion. I thought nothing of it except that I knew it would be a fun, welcome break for him. I did ask him several times if he wanted me to drive him to the airport so he wouldn't have to pay for parking his car, but he insisted on driving himself. He told me, "I" (not "we") "am flying to a friend's house" in NJ, PA, or somewhere, and then, from there, "I" (again, not "we") "am going to West Point with those friends for the reunion." He then told me "I" (remember, first-person singular subject pronoun, "I," NOT 1st person plural, "we") "am flying back to Columbia on Sunday night."

While Jamie was gone, I thought about his return and how I could make it special. On Sunday when he was to return, I had an idea: I would surprise him at the airport to welcome him back to school and back home. Wow! What a great idea! But, because I was raised in the South where ladies didn't "chase" boys or were careful not to appear "forward," I asked my roommates (Beth and Betty) for advice *and* I called my mom to ask her advice. The three of them all thought I was not being too forward and that meeting Jamie at the airport would be a nice gesture.

So, I called the airport, found out the time of his plane's arrival, and set out for the airport. When I got to the gate where his plane would arrive, I met a group of girls who were awaiting their friend's return from a trip. I explained that I was there to surprise Jamie because I knew his return after such a fun weekend away might be a downer. The girls were all saying, "Oh, how sweet. Well, show us who he is when the plane gets here." I was glad to show them who he was (or so I thought)!

As everyone was exiting the plane, I showed the girls who Jamie was, and I noticed that he was talking to a lady. I thought to myself,

"That's just like Jamie ... already made a friend on the plane ... he's so nice ... so friendly." I saw him and exclaimed, "Welcome back!" The girls watching from a distance were smiling, as was I. When Jamie saw me, his eyes widened like saucers. A moment later, two more sets of eyes also widened: mine and the lady's. Imagine the surprise when we all three realized what was going on. Jamie saw me, I saw him and the lady, and the lady saw me. I had no idea that the lady with Jamie was a friend, a *close* friend whom he asked to accompany him to his reunion. The next few seconds were awkward, to say the least! I fumbled for words to say, and eventually, asked them how the weather was in New York (?!?!?), and told Jamie I would see him the next day.

I walked to my car, shocked, and surprised at how naive I was. When I got to my car and realized I had not a cent of money with me, I actually put a fifty-cent parking charge on my credit card, determined *not* to ask Jamie for even a penny to pay the fee. I laughed all the way back to my apartment, deciding I could either laugh or cry, and since I had done nothing wrong, I would laugh.

Thoroughly embarrassed and humiliated, I walked into my apartment where Beth and Betty eagerly awaited good news. They, too, were shocked when I told them what happened. Naturally, I planned to do the only logical, rational thing: I would secretly and quietly withdraw from law school the next day before anyone ever found out about my *faux pas*! I called my mom to tell her the airport story. She was very supportive and encouraged me to stay in school. As Beth and Betty counseled me through this traumatic episode, Beth disappeared for a few minutes. When she returned to the room, she announced, "I've just talked with my dad. I told him what happened, and he says for you to hold your head up and go right back to school. You haven't done anything wrong, so you just keep your head held high." I guess I needed to hear a man's perspective because I did, in fact, go back to school the next day. I thought about his words and realized he was right. I had not done anything wrong. While Jamie hadn't technically done anything wrong, either, he could have forewarned me about another woman! Needless to say, his explanation to his friend didn't go over very well, nor did his explanation to me the next day.

That's when I realized that Jamie and I were coming into this relationship from different points—I was completely single and available; Jamie was not. I was disinterested in dating someone who was seriously involved with another, so the solution was simple for me. I would back out, Jamie and his friend would continue their courtship, get married, and I would not be a home-wrecker. Strangely, though, Jamie's thoughts were that, while he had been seriously involved with this lady, he wasn't sure that she was the "one." He wanted to continue dating, praying for God's guidance about the future.

Over the next two years, we dated on and off, more on than off, but on and off. I loved Jamie, and I knew he was the one for me. I also knew he loved me, and I was the one for him. The problem was that Jamie didn't yet know that he loved me, and I was the one for him. So, during those couple of years, I tried to be patient, praying with Jamie about our relationship. Inwardly, though, I was frustrated by his inability to make a decision, as I saw it.

Eventually, after graduation, I moved to another town to clerk for a judge, Judge Peeples. Jamie and I still saw each other on the weekends, but we didn't have the daily interaction we had had as students. Judge Peeples asked me often about my relationship with Jamie, and his questions caused me to look long and hard at what was taking place. I soon realized that I was spending too much time worrying about whether or not Jamie and I would marry and not enough time getting on with my life. As July 4, 1990, approached, I voiced my frustration to Judge Peeples about my relationship with Jamie. His advice that day was succinct: "Carla," he said, "it's time for Jamie to fish or cut bait!" I, too, had prayed for God's guidance, and while I felt like I knew what God was guiding me (us!) to do, I couldn't impose my wishes on Jamie. Nor did I want to. No woman wants to marry a man unsure about his decision to marry her!

So, on Independence Day, 1990, as Judge Peeples frequently called it later, I told Jamie that our relationship was over. I loved and cared about him very much, but God was leading me to go on with my life. Yes, I was sad, but, yes, God was ever present during that time. I knew that if God wanted us to marry, He would lead Jamie to that decision, but I needed to go forward with my life. I also knew Jamie desired more than anything to follow God and would seek God's guidance with his whole heart. Time and again I had seen him, with God's help, choose to do the harder right rather than the easier wrong. Jamie's character was above reproach. So, I knew that he would do the right thing once God showed him what the right thing was.

Of this I was certain: Jamie's heart's desire was to follow the Lord, be the person God had called him to be, and accomplish the things God called him to accomplish. I took refuge in God's sovereignty and goodness. By God's grace, I was able to go forward joyfully with my life, saddened by my loss, but optimistic about the future. One thing I claimed as truth was this: If Jamie was *not* the man for me, I couldn't wait to meet the man who was … because I knew that if God's best for me was someone other than Jamie, I was in for something (someone!) unbelievable!

Labor Day, 1990, came on uneventfully. I was visiting with my grandmother over that weekend, and I got a phone call. When I answered the phone, it was Jamie. My heart leapt, but I was wondering, "Why is he calling?" He was, as usual, a kind gentleman. Although he was calling to ensure there would be no conflict if he appeared before Judge Peeples for a preliminary hearing the following week, he also asked if he could have dinner with me afterwards. I hesitantly said yes, but I did so because I felt he had his answer to our relationship question.

On the day of his hearing before Judge Peeples, I was anxious and more than a little excited. I had not spoken or seen Jamie for over two months. When I saw him my heart again leapt. Although I didn't know what God had been leading him to do, I was certain he was a man of courage, honor and integrity, so whatever the answer, it would be the right thing.

After dinner, we took a walk. As we did, he asked me if I would go with him to West Point to visit some friends and watch an Army football game. My immediate response was, "No." I had spent two months leaning on God's strength to get over my feelings for Jamie … why would I consider going on a weekend trip with him? He insisted, but I refused. When he asked why I wouldn't go, I told him the frank truth: Unless he and I were getting married, there was no reason for us to spend any time together. That's when he told me that the Lord had shown him that I was the one he was to marry. He told me for the first time that he loved me, that he was in love with me, and that he wanted to marry me. I was blown away! Shock. Elation. Incredulity. Thankfulness. All kinds of emotions were happening at once.

I really was surprised, but I knew God was the author of it all. The next two blissful hours were spent talking about our future and how God revealed His plan to Jamie. We planned to get engaged over Thanksgiving weekend when all of our family would be home. That would be a great time to share our engagement with everyone. Little did I know that Jamie had already planned otherwise.

As the weekend approached for us to visit his friends at West Point, I secretly began planning our wedding. I knew many of the things I wanted, didn't want, and so on, but it was exciting now to begin allowing them into my conscious thoughts. I didn't know that Jamie, too, was secretly planning some things. He had asked me, "Who do I need to ask permission from to marry you?" I jokingly said, "My father, my mother, my grandmother, and Judge Peeples." I found out later that Jamie had scurried around before our trip to ask permission—in person—from everyone on the list!

When Jamie and I left for the weekend, we first flew to New York and stayed with his sister, Lisa, who lived on Long Island. The next day we took one of her cars and drove to West Point where we stayed with some friends, George and Linda. Once we settled in, Jamie told

George and Linda that we were going out for dinner, but he never invited them to join us. I thought that was strange, especially for Jamie, who usually included everyone in dinner invitations. We ate dinner that evening at the Hotel Thayer, an historic hotel on the West Point base. I thoroughly enjoyed dinner at such a beautiful place! Jamie, however, seemed a little puny. Several times he excused himself from our table, and later, I realized he was in the men's room each time (nerves?).

After dinner we took a walk around West Point. Jamie showed me some of the incredible sites there, such as Flirtation Walk and Trophy Point. As we walked, we held hands and just enjoyed being together. I wore a birthstone ring on my left-hand ring finger, and Jamie often twisted and played with it while we held hands. That night, October 5, 1990, he also slipped off my birthstone ring and without my knowledge, slipped on a different ring. All of a sudden I realized what he had done. He immediately knelt on one knee and asked me to marry him! "Well," I said, "I'll have to think about it." *Not!* Of course I said yes, and I'm sure everyone heard the squeals and screams I made. We talked about wedding dates and plans, and eventually, went back to George and Linda's house where we called everyone we could to share our news.

Six months later, on April 6, 1991, we married at Lake City First Baptist Church. Our wedding was perfect in my eyes, although a videotape of the wedding captured two funny events: my ring-bearer's sobbing walk down the aisle and my brother's stellar catch of one of the candles from the altar candelabra. After a reception in the church's social hall, Jamie and I spent the first night of our honeymoon in the Whitney Hotel in Columbia, South Carolina. The next day we flew to New York and stayed in the city one night. From there we took a train to Lisa's house where we once again borrowed one of her cars, drove to the end of Long Island, and took a ferry to New London, Connecticut. We drove to Chatham, Massachusetts, where we spent the first of several nights in a bed-and-breakfast inn. We then went to Martha's Vineyard and stayed in the Charlotte Inn on the island for several more days.

Before flying back to South Carolina, we planned to stay our last night with Lisa and her family on Long Island. When we arrived at Lisa's house, we were wonderfully greeted by her three precious children: Bradley, Samantha, and Jonathan. When bedtime came for all of us, Samantha wanted to sleep with Jamie and me. Of course we said, "Yes." To this day, Jamie enjoys telling people that he is probably the only man in the world whose four-year-old niece slept with him and his bride on their honeymoon! He's probably right, but what a special memory for us.

We've been married almost eighteen years, and I can honestly say that the "wait" for Jamie was worth every moment. I've been abundantly blessed with a Godly husband, a man whom I *know* loves me and who proves his love daily. I also am deeply grateful for the way he leads our family and fathers our children. He often told me that once he knew God's will for his life regarding marriage and a mate, he would go forward and not look back. He has done just that. I've never doubted for once that we were divinely led into our marriage and that we made the right decision about each other. Our relationship grows sweeter year after year, and I can only imagine how precious it will be after we've been married for twenty-five, forty, or fifty years. I look forward to every single minute of it!

Marriage Tips:

1. Before marriage, seek God with your whole heart, asking Him to show you if a person is the right one to marry.

2. Before and after marriage, seek God first in everything, realizing He'll take care of all the other things: finances, children, job, etc.

3. Make all major decisions together, especially those involving finances, children, and extended family. And, yes, buying boats and four-wheelers, or asking relatives to live with you are all major decisions.

4. Laugh at and criticize yourself more than you laugh at and criticize your spouse.

5. Keep the major things major and the minor things minor, and make

sure you know the difference. For example, connecting regularly with your spouse is major; needing to be right about everything is minor.

6. Try to "out-first" your mate. For example, "Honey, where would you like to eat tonight?" or "Where would you like to eat?" or "I asked you first" or "I chose last time. You get to choose this time."

7. You do the right thing toward your spouse even if your spouse chooses not to do the right thing toward you.

8. Constantly seek to learn all you can about the differences in the way God created men and women.

9. Concentrate on making yourself better: a better wife or husband, better mother or father, better daughter or son, better friend, etc. Recognize that you can't change anyone, including your spouse.

10. Learn what makes your mate feel loved; then, purpose to do as much of it as possible.

11. Be the kind of spouse that you would want to be married to and that you would want to be around.

12. Spend quality time together, making sure your mate knows that, after Christ, he or she is the most important person in your life.

13. Thank your partner frequently for the big and small things he or she does for you.

14. Be honest with yourself, and encourage your spouse to be honest with himself. Only with such honesty will you know what needs to improve in your personal lives and in your marriage.

15. Encourage your spouse to do the right thing, realizing that what is right is not always popular, and what is popular is not always right.

16. Laugh a lot! Enjoy each other! Have fun on the journey!

17. Aspire to inspire self-reflection and self-improvement in your mate.

Therefore be imitators of God as dear children. And walk in love, as Christ also has loved us and given Himself for us, an offering and a sacrifice to God for a sweet-smelling aroma.

--Ephesians 5:1

Our Big Secret

Jimmy and Florinette (Ford) Renfrow
Married February 8, 1953
Florence, South Carolina

One day I was sitting on my front porch when I saw a handsome boy with blonde, curly hair pass by in a stripped-down car. I was about thirteen years old at the time. Later I found out his life's story from a good friend of mine whose family had been neighbors of his several years back. He had been going to visit them when he passed by my house. His name was Jimmy Renfrow, and he was fourteen. He went to school in Nichols, South Carolina, but would be moving to Lake View, South Carolina, that year to play baseball.

After several weeks went by, I was at a ball game, and who should I meet but the boy who was in the "stripped-down" car? I later learned he had converted that car from an old family car, and he wanted to be a racecar driver someday. At the ball game I realized that he had metallic green eyes that matched the color of his family car. That night was the beginning of a special walk down memory lane for two teenagers. Cars, cars, cars! Ball games, ball games, ball games!

Though we were too young to date, we ended up at several parties of mutual friends during the year. Then one day we were old enough to date, but only if we went to Baptist Training Union (BTU) on Sunday night and were home by 9 p.m., or if we went to the movies or a ball game one night each week.

I soon found out he loved animals as I did. My first Christmas gift from him was a blonde, cocker spaniel puppy named Dixie. I gave him a green Jantzen sweater to match his eyes and handkerchiefs monogrammed with an "R" from Razor and Clardy's in Mullins, South Carolina. Both of our families shopped there often. We also realized that both of us had spent many Saturday nights eating hot dogs at Mike's in Mullins, but we had never met. Both of us had eaten out many times at Little Pee Dee Lodge and Bullard's near Mullins. His father and my mother had both been Methodists at one time, but now we were Baptists. I had a cousin who had married his mother's sister. We felt we had a lot in common.

Some qualities I especially liked about Jim included his good manners, his kindness to people as well as animals, and his love for family. He didn't drink or smoke. To me, his only fault was that he drove too fast. We fussed about that all the time.

During the ninth grade Jim went to Camden Military Academy in Camden, South Carolina. He had a good year there, but during that year his father had cancer, so he did not go back the next year. Sometimes while he was at Camden he would "thumb" home, something you would never do today, but it was safe back then. Other times he would drive his truck, which he kept secretly hidden at a friend's house near the Academy. He would put a pillow under his covers at school and would slip away to Lake View for a few hours.

Jim's favorite possession was a yellow Willis Jeepster convertible which his daddy had bought for him. I always wore a scarf because it blew my hair. We fussed about this, too. That car was his greatest pride until he wrecked it. In my fourteenth summer at East Cherry Grove Beach on his birthday, July 4, Jim gave me a ring. He had worked and paid for it himself, secretly. I wear it still today, but I didn't then. This was the beginning of our big secret! Someday we were going to get married.

When I was fifteen and he was sixteen, we decided to go ahead and get married secretly. How could we do that with a 9 p.m. curfew and just a few hours for a date? My father's cousin was Judge of Probate in our county, so marrying in Dillon County was out. We went to Marion County, but no one would give us a license. That day was the first and only day I ever cut school (funny how I still feel guilty about it today). Next, we had the idea to go to Florence, South Carolina, an hour away. Jim played basketball, so we had to go and get back for his game later that evening. We did make it, but a patrolman stopped us. Jim told him his father was sick. He told us to go on but to be careful!

Probate Judge Kenneth Grimsley gave us the license. We didn't know we'd be asked to verify the year of our births to prove we were old enough to get married. We had to have some help with the math!

On Sunday afternoon we were married by Adelaide Clayton with my closest friend and a friend of Jim's with us. Only one other friend knew we were getting married, and she got married the next month.

We didn't know that all marriages were reported in the *Florence Morning News*, a local paper. Soon our secret was out when several people in town read our news in the paper. In those days, no married students were allowed to continue and finish high school. It was seventeen years later when I went back to night school to get my high school diploma. I was then able to work as a teacher's aide and eventually as the town librarian for many wonderful years.

On December 19, 1953, our first little girl was born. For years, Jim worked and also spent time track racing. By 1969 we had eight wonderful children, but our family was in trouble. We were planning to get a divorce, but a miracle happened. The Lord Jesus Christ put our family back together. Jim accepted the Lord as his Savior on April 7, 1970. We were now beginning a new life as a Christian family. To God be the glory! We then had three more wonderful children.

Today we are enjoying forty-nine grandchildren and great-grandchildren. Several years ago, Jim retired after fifty years of working. He had worked as a farmer, carpenter, and plant fixer, and he had even fulfilled his dream of owning and operating his own auto mechanic shop. I also retired after thirty-one years of work.

We are reminded of the words of the poem by Robert Browning: "Grow old along with me! The best is yet to be, the last of life, for which the first was made. Our times are in His hand who saith, 'A whole I planned, youth shows but half; trust God; see all, nor be afraid!' "

Marriage Tips:

1. You can go home again.

2. Build your family life on Jesus Christ so you won't need to.

*Take wives and have sons and daughters; • take wives for your sons, and give • your daughters in marriage, * that they may bear sons and daughters; • multiply there, and do not decrease.*

--Jeremiah 29:6

My Two Great Blessings

Ellis Meredith and Augusta Rose (Williams) Stewart
Married September 3, 1939
Newport News, Virginia

Bob and Augusta Stewart Sommers
Married July 30, 1992
Smithville, Virginia

First Blessing

We were seniors in high school in Newport News, Virginia. We were preparing to graduate in 1938 when we met on a field trip to Colonial Williamsburg, organized by our home economics teacher.

Ellis worked in a grocery store before school, after school, and all day Saturdays. He hoped to save enough to pay seventy-five dollars for a 1929 Model A Ford. Boys seldom had a car in those days. John, Ellis's close friend, and Ellis had hoped to drive the Ford to Williamsburg and take several girl classmates along. Our teacher had other plans for them. She assigned the boys and two girls she picked to ride in another car, which was newer and more reliable. I was one of those girls. I got into the backseat with the boys and we hit it off immediately. I am quite a talker and soon learned that John was in a steady relationship with another girl. Ellis was new to the dating game as was I. I learned that we lived in the same neighborhood and attended the same church, but Ellis did not attend regularly as Sunday was his only free day. I never noticed him at school or church as he was very shy and low key.

We really enjoyed the day ride together and he asked me for a date. I had never before had a serious date nor had he. Since many homes did not have telephones, he arranged to send me a note by another of his friends who was dating my next-door neighbor.

I got home starry eyed and told my mother that I had just met the nicest boy. He told me later that he said exactly the same thing to his mom. He sent me the promised note asking me to go to the movies with him. I was delighted but my strict mother declared that I could not go on a date in a car alone with him. We would have to leave his Ford at my home and walk to the streetcar line and ride the short distance downtown to the theatre. There went my wonderful dating plans! I got up the nerve to tell her that if I could not ride in his car, I would rather cancel the date. When she realized that I was serious, she relented. Ellis came to meet her and my father first. She still did not trust us enough, demanding that we come "straight home." She would eventually see the great man Ellis was destined to be.

With that rocky beginning our love and companionship grew. We finished high school and I was well equipped to meet the business world and got a job in a local department store as the office assistant at five dollars per week including Saturdays. Jobs were hard to find, and I was delighted to go to work. Ellis was making twenty-five dollars per week in his job.

We were dating regularly by then and usually went to the movies or for rides in his car. The one date I remember well was a Sunday afternoon when we double-dated and went for a ride at the local beach where the boys used the wet sand as a challenge for driving. Ellis was showing off when he managed to sink his Ford to the hubcaps in sand. The tide came in and covered the wheels and the motor twice before he could get enough help the next day to dig his car out of the sand. When he turned on the key, the motor started and he was able to drive it home. (He later sold the car to a man who wanted the motor for a boat.)

Ellis's troubles were compounded that fateful beach day as he had to find transportation home for both of us girls. Since young people frequented the beach, he gratefully had little trouble finding someone he knew to take us home. The "hubcaps in the sand" was a very exciting date.

Ellis and I were making slow plans for our marriage in the foreseeable future. He gave me a modest diamond ring. The owner of the department store where I worked railed at me about making plans to marry at my young age. I got cold feet and returned the ring to Ellis reluctantly in a quagmire of indecision.

He had had a very different childhood than I. His father died of pneumonia at age thirty-six when Ellis was only seven years old. His mother had been twenty-six, left with a farm she could not manage, a new country home, and farm animals. She tried living in Richmond and working in a tobacco factory but could not adjust to doing such confining indoor work after being raised on a farm with three sisters. She was the cook for the family at an early age and was a remarkably good cook who could stretch a budget. It was necessary that she remarry as she had no other skills and a little boy to raise. Her in-laws, the Stewarts, were a well established family of Scottish stock and were farmers, merchants and businessmen.

She met the brother of a cousin's husband and married him when Ellis was ten. The stepfather worked in the heavy shipbuilding industry in Newport News. The work was very difficult.

The couple had four children in the first five years of marriage. Ellis's mother persevered and raised a nice family. She was a wonderful woman who I loved dearly. Ellis was not very close to his stepfather and began to support himself at age fourteen by working in a grocery store. He realized early on that he needed to be responsible for himself and met the challenge. He was the first of his siblings to graduate from high school, which was a challenge when he went to work before and after school and all day Saturdays.

He persisted and begged me to take back my ring and marry him, which I did later do. We married earlier than we had planned as he had to find a new place to live. By that time my mother had relented in her opinion of Ellis and offered us a bedroom in my parent's home if we married. We were married on Labor Day, Sunday, September 3, 1939, in my pastor's home with our families present. We had bought our first furniture, a bedroom suite, for cash, to use in our new bedroom. We never bought anything during our marriage of forty-six years that was not paid for on the spot except payments on our home(s).

Ellis told me from the beginning that he could not talk "sweet talk" and at one time brought me the printed lyrics to a popular song that went something like this: "I don't want to set the world on fire but just to start a flame in your heart," by Eddie Seiler. That was touching and I loved the gesture.

After getting married at 9 a.m., we went for an overnight honeymoon in Richmond, Virginia. He had borrowed a cousin's car and as we left town, the car radio announced that Great Britain, France, Australia, and New Zealand had declared war on Hitler and Germany. We knew a new world had begun in many ways for us. We understood the uncertainty of our future and lived with my parents for two years. He was earning twenty-five dollars weekly and I was making twelve dollars weekly in a new job at the local Chevrolet dealership. We felt we could face the future together.

My health became an urgent issue when I had a very toxic thyroid problem and needed immediate surgery. I was so ill that treatment had to be planned as a two-step procedure. Surgery was not the surer plan as it is today. No local anesthesia was given. They could not keep me under sedation to take out enough of the diseased gland. After several months I went through surgery again and finally recovered. Ellis paid cash for the surgery and never complained about the extra expense. He was really a faithful and attentive husband. I needed his emotional support for that stressful time. He was always dependable even if he could not say the "sweet words."

When Pearl Harbor was attacked on December 7, 1941, Ellis was called up for duty but was rejected. That is a long story in itself. By April 1942 we were able to afford a three-room apartment and we furnished it. By 1945 we were parents of a beautiful baby girl and delighted Ellis's family with the first grandchild. Our first house cost fifteen hundred dollars, but was a makeover project.

Ours was a typical marriage of that time, for the "greatest genera-tion" had returned from WWII and were buying homes and estab-lishing families. We knew at that time that we would have to work at our marriage. While we never had any big arguments, we had to work together and get along to be happy and successful.

Moving along in time, my dear Ellis passed away in 1985 at the age of sixty-six. My sister reminded me that though he had passed away early, he accomplished all his goals. We had lived a good and happy life together. We never thought of divorce and only loved each other. He was a fine Christian. He liked my friends and work partners. His family had become my dear family as well.

Second Blessing

Bob came into my life in 1987 when our high school class planned its fiftieth-year reunion. Our lives had not crossed in forty-nine years as we lived in adjoining cities. We were both asked by other class-mates to be on the planning committee for the reunion. We had not dated in high school but we did remember each other.

By 1987 I had been widowed for two years and Bob's wife, Gerry, was suffering from cancer. We had the reunion at the Country Club in Newport News, Virginia, in August 1988, and I did not see him again until 1991 when he attended a support group meeting, the Mended Hearts, at our local hospital in Newport News. I had been instrumental in organizing that group with the help of many volunteers in my position of program director for the local chapter of the American Heart Association. I was very surprised to see him and found that he had undergone emergency heart surgery in Florida while attending an antique automobile show. Bob later learned to train Mended Hearts patients because he was so impressed with the way he had been encouraged and helped during his hospitalization. He called his local hospital when he returned home and a volunteer area of his life began.

The hospital's Mended Hearts banquet celebration is when I saw him and his wife, Gerry, again. Gerry was in her final stages of her five-year battle with cancer. Bob was a very devoted husband and the wonderful father of two grown children, two daughters. He was also a grandfather of three. Bob was taking care of Gerry in their home in Smithfield, Virginia, by himself. They loved each other very much and had been married forty-eight years when she died on May 9, 1991.

Some time after Gerry's death, Bob called me and asked me out to dinner. I was glad to go and get to know an old acquaintance, so I agreed. He arrived with a dozen red roses and our first date was a nervous but nice one. Our evening was interesting as he filled me in on his past. Bob left his position as a draftsman in a shipyard to work in space exploration in the 1940s. He was involved with the first seven astronauts at the exciting beginning of space exploration. He flew with them frequently from Hampton, Virginia, to Cape Canaveral, Florida. He retired from NASA as a structural engineer at age fifty-five in 1976.

Gerry and Bob had bought nearly three acres of woodland on a large lake in Smithfield in 1970-71 and built their dream home. He assisted with building it and later added a two-story barn garage that could house eleven cars on site. Yes, he had a passion for antique cars.

As time went by, Bob proposed marriage. We had an unusual series of dates set. We had a private marriage in the chapel of the Trinity United Methodist Church on July 30, 1992, conducted by his pastor, Reverend Wilford Mayton, who had counseled us. We reaffirmed our vows in a simple garden wedding in my backyard in Hampton, Virginia, on August 22, 1992, when our families were free to come. Later, we again repeated our vows in Cana of Galilee on our trip to the Holy Land. We had a honeymoon after our second wedding in the historical town of Edenton, North Carolina, and went there several times in later years because it meant so much.

My world changed completely when we married. I had a nice home in Hampton, but soon realized that I belonged in Smithfield with Bob. We refurbished his home with carpeting, paint, and much elbow grease. We combined our furniture and it was a very comfortable home. We were so happy to welcome my daughter, Sally, and her husband, Bill, of Fernandina Beach, Florida, and Bob's two daughters, Kay (and husband, Fred) of Manassas, Virginia, and Carol (and husband, Don) of Atlanta, Georgia. Our girls melded well and we were blessed with five grandchildren and eight great-grandchildren (now). We loved to travel frequently. We were a geographically scattered family so we visited as often as possible. Bob and I were alone in Smithfield, which in some ways brought us closer.

We traveled to the Holy Land and took the Rhine River cruise in Vienna, Austria. We traveled to the Netherlands; Bruges, Belgium; Alaska; Calgary in Alberta, Canada; Vancouver in British Columbia; Colorado; Wyoming; Yellowstone Park; and Las Cruces, New Mexico (we visited Bob's father's side of the family).

We visited Newton Grove, North Carolina, so I could be introduced to Gerry's family. Bob loved to tell the story of his first trip to Newton Grove when he first met Gerry. He was asked to return thanks at the table in her family's home. His father and uncle had usually done this as he was growing up. Bob was scared speechless when asked and all he could remember to say was, "God is great, God is good...." and was dying of embarrassment when someone noticed his plight and came to his rescue. He had a good sense of humor and laughed at himself after that.

Perhaps one of the best events we planned together was a celebration of our married years. In 1998 Bob wanted to have a party. He had been married forty-eight years and I had been married forty-six years and this would be our sixth anniversary. Since that totaled one hundred years, he said, "Let's go for a celebration. We won't make fifty anyway." We invited at least a hundred family members and friends to a "pig pickin'" catered in our backyard on August 22. On the invitation were the words of the English poet, Robert Browning, "Come walk with me, the best is yet to be; the last of life for which the first was made." Our theme was the song, "The Second Time Around," by Sammy Cahn and Jimmy Van Heusen. Our party was a huge success and we spoke of it often, remembering our fun times together.

Our twelve and a half years together were often spent at home recounting our early years when we had not known each other. I had been a business woman until Ellis's death. Those evenings with Bob were precious and we often quoted poetry that we remembered from our college entrance English class. One of us would start and the other would finish the quote. We had a peaceful, loving, and fulfilling life and appreciated each other. Bob's health eventually slowed him down when he turned eighty but he still remained as active as he could. He died on December 6, 2004, of a stroke while awaiting treatment at the Medical College Hospital in Richmond, Virginia. It was a shocking loss and I still miss him.

I can affirm that you can be in love as deeply at seventy as at seventeen years of age. I have experienced both. Life has been great and full of surprises. I have had a wonderful life and God has blessed me in so many ways that I cannot count them all. I am grateful for my entire life, even now at eighty-seven and living in an assisted living facility.

Marriage Tips:

1. Treat your mate as you wish to be treated.

2. Don't go to bed mad with each other.

3. Avoid credit purchases. If you cannot pay by the end of the month, don't buy it!

4. Travel as extensively as you can afford. See new places and things.

5. Thank God for your children as they are gifts to you from God.

The formula for a happy marriage? It's the same as the one for living in California: When you find a fault, don't dwell on it.

-- Jay Trachman, humorist

Slipping the Sand from My Pocket

Jeffrey and Leah (Graham) Stewart
September 3, 2005
Bar Harbor, Maine

In the summer of 1999, Leah and her two best friends (Kay and Marlee) decided to have an adventure over the summer to reconnect. They had each attended different schools for their first year of college. The prospects for this "adventure" ranged from going out West together to work on a dude ranch or moving to an island in Maine to work at a kayak and bicycle company. It just so happened that a friend's family had purchased a kayak shop a couple of years prior in Bar Harbor, Maine, and it was decided this would be their work destination. The girls packed up their belongings and sent them ahead.

They formed a caravan of giddy girls and Marlee's mom for the trip to Maine.

I managed one of the shops that the Tucker family owned. It offered kayak and canoe rentals, in addition to the bicycle tours that were popular. This offering of the canoe and kayak rentals meant that people working for this shop, in particular, must have decent upper body strength. The boats weighed between forty and one hundred pounds and must be lifted overhead onto car carriers.

On the day I first met the girls, I had pulled up in front of the main store to restock some retail supplies. As I made my way through the front of the store, Marty, the general manager for the store, stopped me and pointed to the trio and said, "These girls are from the Tuckers' home town, Camden, South Carolina, and they are going to be here for the summer." I glanced over, finding a much needed break from the native females of Bar Harbor. ☺

The three new girls brought a fond memory of other Southern girls visiting this New England town. They all waved, but stayed huddled together like a shoal of fish, flashing looks to each other and whispering among themselves. To be honest I really only took this in for a few seconds, then I hurried along to get the supplies I needed for the other shop. It wasn't until much later that the girls told me they thought I was "pretty much a jerk." ☹ I attribute this to my not stopping to "chat it up," but regardless we all moved past my faux pas.

That evening when I spoke to Marty he asked me which one of the girls I would like to hire for my shop. After some discussion we went for a couple of trial days with each of them to see who was most "fit." Leah was the most unlikely fit because at five feet four inches, one hundred ten pounds, I figured that there was no way she could handle a one-hundred-pound boat above her head. As luck and a little interest from upper management would have it, she ended up in the position. Now, I'm not saying that I was interested (☺) but she fit well with everyone; we all worked well together, there was good chemistry, and she had the ability/willingness to learn.

After a busy summer it was time for the girls to return to their respective schools. Leah and I got along very well, but it was a great friendship and nothing more. When we were saying goodbye for the summer, she said, "I will see you later, I know this isn't goodbye." This was a typical, sweet comment from her, but she also gave me a small card that said how great she thought I was. This card would later be the catalyst for arguments with my then current girlfriend, though it was written only as a nice note.

I flew back to North Carolina from Maine that fall to my father's wedding and I gave Leah a call to invite her. To my surprise she came. We had a great time. Aside from a moment in the airport where we inadvertently held hands just a moment too long for just being good friends (Leah still denies this), it was a quick, fun-filled trip.

Come spring, I enrolled in school at Western Carolina University. Leah and I would chat on AOL instant messenger occasionally, then weekly, then daily. There was a bit of cyber-flirting in retrospect, but at the time I was clueless. I did visit her a few times at the University of Georgia (her alma mater), but there was nothing more than a quick hello/goodbye, here and there.

As the summer approached, Leah and her two girl friends set out on an encore visit to Bar Harbor. I offered to give Kay and Leah a ride to Maine when the time came to go. Fun trip! Enough said!

As the summer went on Leah and I began spending more and more time together. Before either of us knew it, we were ... a bit more than friends. We had an incredible summer together. There is simply no better place on earth to fall in love. I still tease Leah that all the special places I took her were on the local date plan, a list of special events and places those local boys from the island would take girls from out of town to romance them to death. She didn't have a chance!

I ended up in school at the University of Georgia. Leah moved to Jacksonville, Florida, to work after she graduated a year before I was scheduled to do the same. It was in Jacksonville that I proposed to her.

One of our favorite places on earth is a sand beach in Bar Harbor and I had wanted to propose to her there, but financially it wasn't possible, so I did what I could when I thought the time was right. I managed to get a bottle of wine made from the blueberries on an island in Maine. I dropped it off at a Jacksonville restaurant prior to our reservation and had the server offer it to us as a special before dinner. This was great and the look on her face was of complete surprise. After a great dinner I offered a walk along the water. We walked and laughed a lot as we tend to do.

When we got to a good spot and sat on a bench, I had her take her shoes off and I slipped the sand from my pocket and explained that I was unable to take her to "sand beach," but I brought "sand beach" to her. I poured it on the ground and had her put her feet in it, then got on one knee and proposed. Her response was, "Are you kidding?" Then I saw her lower lip quiver which meant it hit home. Little did she know that I had asked permission from Art and Isla (her parents) first.

We decided to get married in Bar Harbor but also to have a later reception in Camden, South Carolina, for those who couldn't make our wedding date. The wedding was incredible. We were married in the heart of downtown Bar Harbor on September 3, 2005, and we had an incredible reception (thanks, Grahams) consisting of a lobster bake and all of our closest friends and family together celebrating on the shore. As the sun started to fall into the water, I asked Leah to walk to the water with me. When we returned everyone had disappeared from the reception. Leah was confused to say the least. As we made our way to the other side of the point, we found everyone gathered around the dock where Andy, a close local friend (and ultimately Kay's husband), was waiting in a dinghy with a smile. We made a toast to all of our friends and family and boarded the dingy to make our way to a sixty-foot sailboat that literally sailed us away into the sunset.

I'm sure that Leah has a completely different account of these happenings, but we can both agree that it's important to hold onto something great when you find it as it promises a lifetime of smiles.

Marriage Tips:
Jeff's tips:

1. Marry your best friend.

2. Laugh.

3. Make her feel beautiful.

Leah's tips:

1. Be patient.

2. Listen.

3. Enjoy the great outdoors together (walk, bike, hike, sit, plant a garden together) with no computers, cell phones, etc.

4. Make time for yourself and each other.

5. Laugh.

6. Marry your best friend.

7. Be president of each other's fan club.

A successful marriage requires falling in love many times, always with the same person.

-- Mignon McLaughlin, author

On Another Guy's Lap
When We Met

Ed and Marlene Strobach
Married January 30, 1954
Upper Darby, Pennsylvania

How Ed and I met is probably as crazy as our whole courtship. I was a freshman in college and already had a boyfriend whose lap I happened to be sitting on when Ed walked into my life. The scene was in a fraternity house on the campus of Drexel University in Philadelphia, Pennsylvania. A friend of mine came into the fraternity house with a friend of his who wanted to meet me because I had "red hair." So they motioned for me to get off my boyfriend's lap and come meet Ed … end of boyfriend, beginning of Ed.

Now the main reason that I wanted to date Ed was because he was in the "right" fraternity. By that I mean he was in the fraternity of athletes — and as many young girls of my age did — we worshipped athletes. (We had a lot to learn, didn't we?)

Well, as Ed and I continued to date, there was one thing that became apparent to me. I could talk to him more easily than I could to any other guy I had ever dated. We could sit for hours over a cup of coffee or lunch in the student union and just talk and talk and talk … and not about surface stuff but meaningful thoughts.

So, we dated for a while and I got "pinned." Ed graduated from college two years ahead of me. I pinned his lieutenant bars on him during his graduation ceremony.

Ed was about to be called into the Army as a result of his commission as a lieutenant in ROTC. There was talk about his being sent to Germany, which is where several of our friends were being sent. Of course, I wanted to go to Germany if Ed went. However, he was not talking "marriage" or even "engagement." So, here comes the proposal. I said to Ed, "If we are not married by the time you go overseas, I will not be here by the time you return."

Needless to say, we got married. And can you believe? We ended up not going to Germany. As a matter of fact, it was to be thirty years before I finally visited Germany.

Marriage Tips:

1. As far as I am concerned, what makes a good marriage is what attracted me to Ed in the first place (no, not the right fraternity☺) … the ability to talk meaningfully.

2. Practice listening.

3. Learn to appreciate each other and work together—even though, in our case, we did not realize that is what we were doing.

4. I only wanted to divorce him once☺. That was because I locked him out when he came home once at 3 in the morning. He knocked the door down. We were young then. ☺

5.   Forgive.
6.   Offer understanding.
7.   Remember in hard times what attracted you to each other.
8.   Fifty-four years of deep love… a great gift.

Love at first sight is easy to understand; it's when two people have been looking at each other for a lifetime that it becomes a miracle.

-- Amy Bloom

By the Ocean

Donnie and Donni Thompson
Married May 23, 1992
Smithville, Georgia

Donnie and I met in 1990 when I worked at Food Lion in Fernandina Beach, Florida. My best friend and his best friend were my fellow workers at the store.

One night Donnie invited me on a date to a fair called Midnight Madness on October 26, 1990. I had to borrow the money to go because I did not know Donnie well. I did not know he would end up wanting to pay for everything. He was generous and kind, I realized. And thus began a very special friendship and I somehow knew that he was going to be someone special in my life.

A few months later, in 1991, Donnie actually proposed to me in his truck near the ocean in Fernandina Beach. We had been having a conversation about his mom as she had asked him if he was close to proposing to me. I said to Donnie, "And what did you say?" He just looked at me and there on the spot he so sweetly asked me to marry him. I actually received my ring on February 14 along with roses and some luscious fudge. I was kind of puzzled by the flowers at the time because he had not given me any before. He kind of looked at me sheepishly and said they came with the ring.

We were engaged for eighteen months while planning our wedding. I ended up living with his parents during this time. I grew to care very much for his family.

Our special day finally arrived on May 23, 1992. We were married in Smithville, Georgia, where my father's home church was at the time. I remember when Donnie and I arrived at the reception after having pictures taken, there was no food left. (I knew that our families enjoyed food and fellowship, which was to become a frequent, family tradition. However, where did all the food go?) It was time for the toast and I thought at first that the punch was gone, too. Luckily earlier, my cousin had seen the punch in the punch bowl getting low and "saved the day" by saving us some. I remember that I was so hungry, but "punch" it was to be.

We honeymooned at Disneyland in Orlando, Florida, for four days. We returned to Fernandina Beach and to a reception given by his parents.

Marriage Tips:

1. God first, family second.

2. The family values that Donnie and I brought to our marriage came from our parents. His parents were married for forty-one years and my parents were married for thirty-three years.

3. Never let anyone tell you that you are not a good parent. Pray for, love, and support your children. Show them love. Discipline is the

key. Make sure they know what you expect from them, such as honesty, courtesy, helpfulness, and good behavior.

4. Donnie is the spiritual head of our household. He took that role early in our marriage.

5. We show affection to our children and most importantly, to each other.

6. The challenges in life make a marriage stronger, not weaker. This was very true when Bryant was seriously ill as a child.

7. Pray. The power of prayer for us has been the key to a strong marriage, as God is our strongest ally.

The critical period in matrimony is breakfast time.

-- A.P. Herbert, English writer

The Winter of 1954

Bob and Jane Turney
Married June 18, 1955
Cleveland, Ohio

The winter of 1954, my senior year in college, I met Bob Turney. He was in his first year of dental school. We both attended what is now Case Western Reserve University in Cleveland, Ohio.

The dorm girls all had meals in the same dining room; he was a waiter for the evening meal. I noticed him so I asked another waiter, George, who he was. They were both dental students and knew each other.

George thought a lot of Bob. Bob was hard to read, though. He just stood quietly near the table with a sly smile, but did not say more than a few words to any of us. My sorority had a party coming up in January, so I invited him to go. I wanted to get to know him. Bob accepted and we went out for coffee one night to get better acquainted.

The sorority party was a typical '50s college affair with lots of laughing, talking, and a few drinks. I was pleased and surprised at his ability to fit in and chat with my friends, and they liked him. From that night on neither of us went out with anyone else. Within a few weeks we both knew that we were a good match. We were both ready for commitment. In the spring he came home with me to meet my family, and they loved him. My little brother named his new electric locomotive "Strong Bob." A while later I went with him to meet his parents.

That summer he went away to work in the steel mill so we only saw each other once. People did not use long distance just to chat in those days, so we wrote letters. I was working and living with a friend in Cleveland.

After school resumed we were able to see each other regularly. He spent nearly every weekend at our house, riding the bus from Cleveland as he had no car. On Wednesday night I drove with a friend to spend a few hours with him. He never did ask me to marry him. He only said, "And I thought I was going to be a bachelor." That was good enough for me. During this time we all got to know each other very well. Over the Christmas holidays we were engaged. We married that summer on June 18, 1955.

My parents had married in an old brick Gothic church and so did we. It was the hottest day of the summer—no air conditioning, of course, and the best man passed out on the long, concrete steps outside the church. As a result Bob had to pick him up and drive to the reception while Ralph recovered.

Our small apartment near the school was old but convenient. We lived very frugally those two years until he finished school. I worked as a home economist during that time; he worked a twelve-hour day on Saturdays, still riding the bus.

After two years in the Air Force we returned to Ohio and he began his dental practice in a beautiful, rural suburb. By this time we had two children. It was a happy time. Two years later we bought a lovely home in which we spent twenty-five years. We had our third child.

I learned as the years went by there were to be good and bad times. Neither of them last forever. I learned that a bad time is not the end of a marriage. Divorce was not an option for us. It seemed to me that life can be a roller-coaster and marriage could be a gamble. Therefore, it is important to find out everything you can about your partner in advance of marriage. There will still be surprises. We, however, had a very blessed marriage.

Marriage Tips:

1. All kinds of issues may appear unexpectedly: financial, health, challenges with family or children.

2. The use of time and money and the management of children can present challenging differences.

3. Honesty and trust are essential. Compromise and forgiveness pave a smoother way.

4. Sharing the tasks of the home and care of children is important. Allow each other time alone for pursuits. Be generous with praise, thanks, and appreciation.

5. Make every effort to be friends with your spouse's parents.

6. Men and women are different in more ways than physical ones. They do not think the same way. Often men are focused on the career, and the women are focused on the family. This can be a cause of frustration and disagreement in the early years. We cannot change these roles, but we can understand and prepare for them.

7. Keep God in your life and talk with Him daily. Live in a way that will be an example to your children.

(It took me most of a lifetime to learn these things. I was blessed to be married to the kind of man I wanted. I lost him three years ago after fifty years of being together.)

Perhaps, after all, romance did not come into one's life with pomp and blare, like a gay knight riding down; Perhaps it crept to one's side like an old friend through quiet ways. Perhaps it revealed itself in seeming prose, until some sudden shaft of illumination fling athwart its pages betrayed the rhythm and the music; Perhaps...perhaps...love unfolded naturally out of a beautiful friendship, as a golden-hearted rose slipping from its green sheath.

-- L.M. Montgomery from Anne of Avonlea

My Folks Liked Him Instantly

Ron and Miriam "Mim" Walker
Married November 2, 1956
Houston, Texas

Ron and I were to have met on a blind date on Thanksgiving, 1953. It didn't happen. I had only had one blind date ever before and wasn't too interested in this one, but decided to help out a friend. The friend was my minister's daughter in Houston, Texas. Long story short, the date didn't happen. I waited for at least an hour that evening and finally called my friend. She told me that she had forgotten to inform Mr. Ron Walker that she had a date for him. He went back to his hotel after having dinner with our minister's family. The only reason he was in Houston this Thanksgiving was that his friend from school was dating our minister's daughter.

About two months later in February 1956, Ron was in Houston again and called my friend to get my name. He called and we were talking and he asked me where I was from. When I told him Beckley, West Virginia, he in turn told me he only knew one person from West Virginia—a fraternity brother, who just happened to be my next-door neighbor. I had even dated him! To say the least, I felt he was an okay guy and accepted a date with Ron.

First impression: he's okay, but not my type. Wasn't tall enough or blond, didn't like his Yankee accent (☺) and more. *But* my folks liked him instantly even though, as I have said, "he was a Yankee." I was dating several other guys at the time and just added Ron to the list whenever his career brought him to Houston. Ron tells everyone that the only time he could date me was after church at dinner as I had to get home in time for another Sunday night date. In the '50s you could date several guys and be considered a "good" girl. Certainly this has not been the case since the '70s when you could only date one person at a time.

Finally, Ron had enough of Sunday dinners or Saturday afternoons at the beach. One Saturday we went out with a couple, one of whom was his friend from the service, who was a pilot in Houston. His friend was giving us rides in his small private plane and unknown to me, Ron had asked his friend to keep me up in the air so that I couldn't get back to Houston in time for a date that evening. Of course, the plane landing was stalled. I didn't dare show up at my house in another man's car with my other date waiting for me. Thank goodness my folks happened to be out of town that weekend or there would have been a worse fiasco! Well, as you can surmise, Ron finally got a Saturday night date with me. He was beginning to appeal a little to me but still I only saw him every couple of weeks.

In May 1956, Ron asked me to go with him to a concert in Dallas for a weekend. Much to my surprise, my folks agreed so we took off in his car that evening and I planned to fly back. I was working in Houston for an oil company, modeling and doing some commercials. In Dallas I met several of his friends, liked them, and they seemed to like me. But much to my chagrin, Ron told me he loved me and was going to marry me. I started saying that he didn't know me nor I him. Fortunately, he wasn't offended.

Anyway, we continued dating whenever he was in Houston until one night he proposed in June 1956. I couldn't give him an answer as I felt I was in love with another person. In July we went with another couple to a boat race at Corpus Christi and on the way home we had sort of a disagreement. Didn't talk for a good hour and all the music on the radio was wailing about not being loved anymore, etc. I finally scooted over to him and said in a low voice, "If you still want to marry me, I accept."

So this meant another trip to Dallas to get the wedding rings. Ron proposed again when he gave me the ring on Lovers Lane in Dallas, Texas, that fateful July.

We were married on Friday, November 2, 1956. I was told that Friday weddings were unlucky. Well, I am here to tell you that we are going strong after fifty-three years this coming November. We were married in the Second Presbyterian Church in Houston with four bridesmaids and four groomsmen, a maid of honor, and a flower girl. The reception was at my family's home, which was lovely. After the reception I changed clothes and Ron said if the car starts we are in luck. Well, we got in the car, waved goodbye and started the car. Ron put the car in reverse and guess what? The car stayed put. His groomsmen had put the car up on cinderblocks! Finally, we were on our way into a long and happy marriage.

We went to Mexico City and Acapulco on our honeymoon. We were there for two weeks and had to call home for money to be wired so we could pay our way home. Yes, we had a ball down there and spent all our money.

After the honeymoon we moved to Dallas, Texas, and lived there until 1960. We moved to Maryland for three years and onward to New Jersey for three more years, we thought. We actually stayed there twenty-five years. Then we moved southward to Florida where we live today. We have four children, seven grandchildren, and one great-grandson.

We were fortunate to repeat our wedding vows in 2006 (our fiftieth anniversary) on a cruise off the coast of Spain with our very best friends.

Marriage Tips:

1. Have lots of conversation.

2. Never go to bed mad, if possible.

3. Be big enough to be the first to say "I'm sorry" and "I love you."

4. Marriage is a lot of hard work and requires one hundred and one percent from each other in good times and in bad.

5. Sex is always important, but there are many other factors that make a marriage work.

6. At times marriage is hard and you need parental support. But when you marry, your parents become secondary. Husband first. I emphasized this, even with my children.

7. Husband first—because children are loaned to you, they get married, they leave, and so goes the circle of life.

A good marriage is not a secret. It is a strategy.
-- Becky Duke, Celebrating Marriage

LaVergne, TN USA
02 December 2009
165576LV00002B/1/P